The Regime of Islands Reframed

The Law of the Sea

Volumes published in this Brill Research Perspectives title are listed at *brill.com/rpls*

The Regime of Islands Reframed

Developments in the Definition of Islands under the International Law of the Sea

By

Clive Schofield

BRILL

LEIDEN | BOSTON

This paperback book edition is simultaneously published as issue 3.1–2 of *The Law of the Sea*, DOI:10.1163/24519359-12340008.

Library Congress Control Number: 2020950989

Typeface for the Latin, Greek, and Cyrillic scripts: "Brill". See and download: brill.com/brill-typeface.

ISBN 978-90-04-44946-6 (paperback)
ISBN 978-90-04-44947-3 (e-book)

This book is printed on acid-free paper and produced in a sustainable manner.

Contents

The Regime of Islands Reframed:

Developments in the Definition of Islands under the International Law of the Sea

Clive Schofield
WMU-Sasakawa Global Ocean Institute, World Maritime University
chs@wmu.se

Abstract

The definition of islands represents a longstanding source of uncertainty under the international law of the sea, resulting in numerous disputes among coastal States. This is primarily due to the significant impacts the legal status of islands has on both their maritime entitlements and potential role in the delimitation of maritime boundaries. This study highlights the geographical diversity of islands and outlines the historical development of as well as progress towards the clarification of the legal definition of islands. The Award of the Arbitral Tribunal in the South China Sea case is examined in detail as it provides the first detailed international judicial examination and interpretation of the Regime of Islands. The definition of other types of insular features including low-tide elevations and artificial islands as well as submerged features are also addressed. Reactions to the interpretation of Article 121 by the Tribunal in the South China Sea case are explored before conclusions and considerations on the potential implications of these developments are offered.

Keywords

islands – rocks – low-tide elevations – artificial islands – submerged features – South China Sea

1 Introduction

Islands come in a vast array of shapes and sizes, from, as it were, mere 'flyspecks on the map' of miniscule dimensions, to the world's largest island, Greenland,

 | DOI:10.1163/9789004449473_002

or even the 'island continent' of Australia.[1] Insular features also go by many names – islands, islets, rocks, reefs, atolls, cays, banks, shoals, sandbanks and low-tide elevations. Further, islands are composed of a wide range of materials with radically different physical characteristics as well as elevations. For example, islands can be high, rocky features that change extremely slowly. Alternatively, islands may be composed of low-elevation and far more readily formed and eroded sediments, such as sand, silt and mud which may be constantly shifting location, or may be ephemeral in character, forming and disappearing above and below sea level cyclically in response to the deposition or accretion of material and as a consequence of erosive forces.

Islands exist throughout the global ocean and thus across the world's full latitudinal and climatic range, from the vicinity of the equator to the high Polar latitudes. Islands therefore have an extremely broad range of vegetation cover, availability of water and prevailing temperatures. Further, insular features may also be located in close proximity to mainland coasts or be remote from mainland shores. The physical characteristics of islands, in terms of their size, geological composition and elevation, coupled with their location geographically, climatically and environmentally, necessarily have important implications for the formation and erosion of islands and their persistence as well as habitability over time.

The definition of islands and thus determination of the maritime entitlements associated with them has proved to be an enduring source of dispute between coastal States world-wide. This is primarily because of the implications of these issues for the spatial extent of coastal State maritime claims, and thus rights over valuable marine resources, and with respect to the potential role of islands in the delimitation of maritime boundaries. Here it can be noted that the presence, or, indeed, merely the perceived presence, of valuable marine resources within the maritime areas that can potentially be claimed from islands remains a potent driver for maritime disputes.

Clarifying the legal definition of islands is therefore an essential aspect in determining the extent of maritime limits and boundaries, rights over marine resources, as well as responsibilities related to the safeguarding of marine environment within zones of maritime jurisdiction. Consequently, defining islands and their maritime entitlements has important implication for realising blue

1 Greenland, with an area of 2,175,600 km^2, is generally acknowledged as the largest island in the world. Australia, with an area of 7,692,000 km^2, is usually considered to be a continental landmass. Australian government sources refer to Australia as "the smallest of the world's continents" whilst simultaneously terming the country "an island nation". See, Australian Government, 'The Australian Continent', available from https://www.australia.gov.au/about-australia/our-country/the-australian-continent.

economic opportunities, good ocean governance and international peace and security.

This study focuses on the issue of developments in the definition of various types of insular features under the international law of the sea with particular reference to recent developments. The historical development of the definition of islands under the international law of the sea is briefly explored and the drafting history of the 'Regime of islands' under the United Nations Convention on the Law of the Sea (LOSC) outlined.[2] The unanimous Award of the Arbitration Tribunal in the case between the Philippines and China[3] where it pertains to issues related to the definition of insular status is then detailed, as it provides the first international judicial interpretation of, and thus reframes, the regime of islands under the LOSC. Reactions to the South China Sea Tribunal's Award are then outlined and appraised. Concluding thoughts are offered with particular consideration as to the degree to which the regime of islands under international law has been clarified, what scope for flexibility in interpretation as well as what uncertainties remain regarding the definition of islands. The potential implications of these developments both within and beyond the South China Sea are considered and reflections on potential future developments offered.

2 Defining Islands

2.1 *International Legal Categorisation of Insular Features*

The definition and maritime entitlements of islands under the international law of the sea are dealt with under the LOSC. The Convention provides the generally accepted legal framework governing the global ocean including maritime jurisdictional claims, limits and boundaries.[4] In accordance with the LOSC, the breadth of a coastal State's claims to territorial sea, contiguous zone and exclusive economic zone (EEZ) are measured from baselines

2 See, United Nations Convention on the Law of the Sea (Montego Bay, 10 December 1982, in force 16 November 1994) 1833 *UNTS* 396, [hereinafter LOSC or the Convention].

3 South China Sea Arbitration, Philippines v China, Award, PCA Case No 2013–19, ICGJ 495 (PCA 2016), 12 July 2016, Permanent Court of Arbitration [PCA] [hereinafter, the South China Sea Arbitration, Award]. Both the Tribunal's Award and its Award on Jurisdiction and Admissibility [hereinafter, South China Sea Arbitration, Award on Jurisdiction] are available on the website of the Permanent Court of Arbitration, available from https://pca-cpa.org, at https://pcacases.com/web/view/7.

4 At the time of writing 167 States (plus the European Union) had become parties to the LOSC.

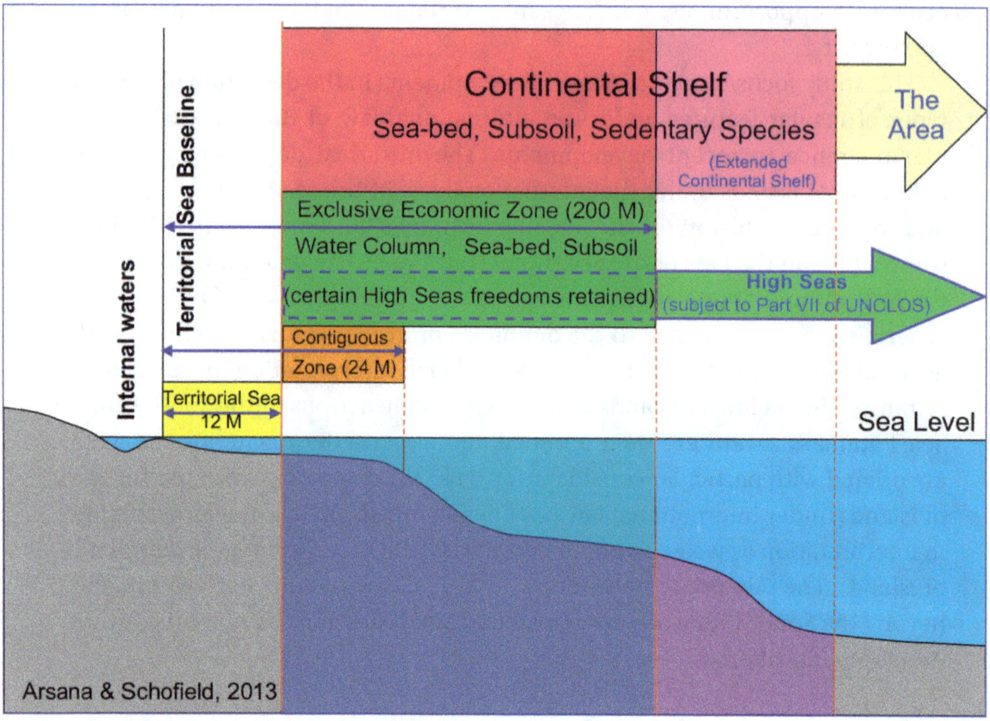

FIGURE 1 Baselines and Claims to Maritime Jurisdiction
SOURCE: SCHOFIELD AND ARSANA[5]

along the coast as follows to no further than 12, 24 and 200 nautical miles (M) respectively (see Figure 1).[6]

The great geographical diversity of islands is encompassed in the international law of the sea under the LOSC by a relatively limited array of types or categories of insular feature, namely islands and rocks (Article 121), low-tide elevations (Article 13) and artificial islands (Article 60(8)).[7] Distinguishing between different categories of insular feature, especially between islands that

5 International Hydrographic Organization (IHO) A Manual on Technical Aspects of the United Nations Convention on the Law of the Sea - 1982 (TALOS), Special Publication No.51, 5th edition, (International Hydrographic Bureau: Monaco, 2014), Figure 5.1, Chapter 5, 3.

6 LOSC, Articles 3 and 4, 33(2), and 57. It is acknowledged that delineating the outer limits of the continental shelf in accordance with Article 76 of the LOSC where this limit lies seawards of 200 M EEZ limits is a substantially more complex task. However, distance measurements, notably the 200 and 350 M limits, remain important, however. See, for example, PJ Cook and CM Carleton (eds), *Continental Shelf Limits* (Oxford University Press: Oxford, 2000).

7 See, for example, DH Anderson, 'Some Aspects of the Regime of Islands and the Law of the Sea' (2017) 32 *International Journal of Marine and Coastal Law* 316–331, at 319.

can generate the full suite of maritime entitlements and rocks which cannot has, however, proved to be a long-standing conundrum for the international law of the sea community.

This Section summarises historical developments in the definition of islands prior to consideration of the drafting history of Article 121 of the Convention. The regime of islands under the LOSC is then outlined, including consideration of the key requirements for insular status. Subsequent progress towards the interpretation and clarification of Article 121 of the LOSC with reference to State practice and international jurisprudence is explored and the extensive scholarly literature on this issue touched on. A later Section is devoted to low-tide elevations and artificial islands, installations and structures (see Section 4).

2.2 *Historical Developments in the Definition of Islands*

2.2.1 Early Codification Efforts

The international legal definition of islands first arose as an issue in the course of the Hague Codification Conference of 1930.[8] Although this conference did not prove to be a success, in the course of these discussions a distinction was drawn between permanent elevations of the seabed which were to be disqualified from the definition of islands on the one hand, and low-tide elevations which were to be denied a territorial sea in their own right but which were potentially valid basepoints for measuring its breadth on the other.[9] The draft definition of islands read as follows: "An island is an area of land, surrounded by water, which is permanently above the high-water mark."[10]

The issue was taken up in the 1950s by the International Law Commission (ILC) with the draft definition of 1930 used as a basis for discussions.[11] It was suggested that the words "normal circumstances" be inserted before "permanently above the high-tide mark" in order to address exceptional situations where an insular feature might be wholly inundated. During the first United Nations Conference on the Law of the Sea (UNCLOS I), the United States proposed alternative wording excluding the reference to normal circumstances.[12]

8 HW Jayewardene, *The Regime of Islands in International Law* (Martinus Nijhoff: Dordrecht, 1990), at 3.

9 Ibid., at 4.

10 Report of the Second Commission (Territorial Waters) of the Hague Codification Conference, Report of Sub-Committee II. See, Report of the Second Commission, L.N. Doc. C.230, M.117, 1930 V., 13, cited in ibid., at 4.

11 Ibid.

12 Ibid., at 4–5.

This was accepted and became the basis for the first paragraph of Article 10 of the 1958 Convention on the Territorial Sea and Contiguous Zone.[13]

With regard to the maritime zonal entitlements of islands, the usage of islands in territorial sea claims meant that, by the time of the 1930 Hague Codification Conference, the suggestion that each island should possess its own territorial sea was uncontroversial.[14] The ILC accepted the capacity of islands to generate maritime claims and this position was also agreed during UNCLOS I. Consequently, Article 10 of the Convention on the Territorial Sea and Contiguous Zone of 1958 reads as follows:

1. An island is a naturally formed area of land, surrounded by water, which is above water at high tide.
2. The territorial sea of an island is measured in accordance with the provisions of these articles.

2.2.2 The Drafting History of Article 121 of the LOSC

The drafting history of Article 121 of the LOSC has been subject to substantial scholarly attention and these discussions need not be recounted in exorbitant detail here. Nonetheless, the discussions leading to the formulation of Article 121 needs to be addressed here as it is an important supplementary means for understanding the intent of the drafters of the article.[15]

While examinations of the records of the discussions leading to the drafting of Article 121 of the LOSC make it clear that Article 121(3) was intended to limit the impact of some features from generating broad maritime zones, they also provide ample evidence of a substantial diversity of views that the issue of islands provoked.[16] In particular, while some States were keen to minimise

---

13 Convention on the Territorial Sea and Contiguous Zone, opened for signature 29 April 1958, 516 UNTS 205 (entered into force 10 September 1964).

14 Ibid., at 9–12. See also, Jayewardene (n 8), at 9–10.

15 Where the terms of a treaty are ambiguous or obscure, Article 32 of the Vienna Convention on the Law of Treaties (VCLT) provides that supplementary means of interpretation may be used where the meaning of treaty terms is unclear and this may include "the preparatory work of the treaty and the circumstances of its conclusion." See, VCLT, 23 May 1969 1155 UNTS 331 (entered into force 27 January 1980), Articles 31 and 32.

16 See, United Nations, *United Nations Conferences on the Law of the Sea, Official Records, Third Conference* (Williams, Hein & Co: Buffalo, NY, 1980, reprinted 2000). See also, United Nations, Division for Ocean Affairs and the Law of the Sea, *Régime of islands: Legislative history of Part VIII (Article 121) of the United Nations Convention on the Law of the Sea* (United Nations: New York, 1988); and SN Nandan and S Rosenne (eds) *United Nations Convention on the Law of the Sea 1982: A Commentary*, Volume III (Kluwer Law International: Dordrecht, 1995), at 321–339.

the impact of small islands on claims to maritime jurisdiction, others had an interest in maximising maritime jurisdictional claims from such insular features. Indeed, many of the key contributors to the debates on the question of islands at the Third United Nations Conference on the Law of the Sea (UNCLOS III) had specific national concerns relating not only to the potential capacity of small islands to generate extensive claims to maritime jurisdiction, but the potential impact of such features on the delimitation of maritime boundaries with their maritime neighbours.[17]

What became the final text of Article 121 was proposed at the third session of UNCLOS III in 1975 in response to the President of UNCLOS III's requirement that the chairs of the committees making up the Conference produce a single negotiating text.[18] Paragraph one of the 1975 draft text incorporated the text of Article 10 of the 1958 Convention on the Territorial Sea and Contiguous Zone verbatim. Paragraph two restated the principle that the maritime zones of islands were to be determined in the same manner as for other land territory.[19] The controversial third paragraph appears to have been adapted, at least in part, from Romania's proposals regarding islets and small islands.[20] It has been observed that the draft text of 1975 was essentially distilled from a document outlining the main trends in the discussions of the Second

17 Notably, Romania, Turkey and Denmark were keen to minimise the maritime claims and role in maritime delimitation of certain islands, States such as Greece and Venezuela were determined to safeguard their maritime claims from their islands. See, for example, JRV Prescott and CH Schofield, *Maritime Political Boundaries of the World*, 2nd edition (Martinus Nijhoff: Leiden/Boston, 2005), at 65–75; and, R Beckman and CH Schofield, 'Moving Beyond Disputes over Island Sovereignty: ICJ Decision Sets Stage for Maritime Boundary Delimitation in the Singapore Strait' (2009) 40 *Ocean Development and International Law* 1–35, at 9–10.

18 Article 132 of the Informal Single Negotiating Text of 1975 proposed by Reynaldo Galindo Pohl, of El Salvador, Chairman of the Second Committee of UNCLOS III at the time. See, United Nations, 1980 (A/CONF.62/WP8/Part II). See also, Nandan and Rosenne (n 16), at 335. Franckx notes that as Chairman Pohl, was hospitalised for most of the relevant session of the conference, so the drafting of what became Article 121(3) of the LOSC fell to the committee's rapporteur Satya N. Nandan and his colleague Gudmundur Eriksson. See, E Franckx, 'The Arbitral Tribunal's interpretation of paragraph 2 in Article 121: a first but important step forward', in S Jayakumar, T Koh, R Beckman, T Davenport and HD Phan (eds), *The South China Sea Arbitration: The Legal Dimension* (Edward Elgar: Cheltenham, 2018), 154–175, at 158.

19 The scope of the draft article was also narrowed to exclude any provisions on islands held by colonial powers and their role in the delimitation of maritime boundaries. See, Prescott and Schofield (n 17), at 335.

20 Ibid., at 335.

Committee of UNCLOS III and "was intended to serve solely as a starting point for further negotiations."[21]

The 1975 draft text remained unchanged through subsequent negotiating documents, though this was not for lack of trying. A variety of amendments were proposed with a view to introducing a degree of specificity and objective tests to the regime of islands. These proposals related to a range of factors including island size, proximity to mainland coasts, composition, presence of water and population.[22] Additionally, proposals were made to delete the third paragraph of the draft article entirely and to deal with the impact of islands on the delimitation of maritime boundaries.[23] Ultimately, all of the proposed amendments to the then draft Article 121 foundered and the regime of islands emerged unchanged, essentially because of the impossibility of formulating an alternative provision that would reconcile divergent views and deliver consensus on a particularly controversial issue.[24] This outcome also reflected the challenges of achieving a general rule applicable to highly diverse islands occurring throughout the global ocean.

The precise interpretation of the island/rock distinction was thus left to the future for the sake of achieving broad agreement on the LOSC – detailed interpretation that has now been provided by the Tribunal in the South China Sea arbitration case (see Section 3). LOSC also includes provisions relating to low-tide elevations (Article 13) and artificial islands (Article 60(7–8)) (see Section 4).

2.3 *The Regime of Islands under the LOSC*

The somewhat grandiosely titled "Regime of islands", comprises a distinct part (Part VIII) of the LOSC yet consists of but a single Article, Article 121 of the Convention, comprising three paragraphs as follows:

21 See, Franckx (n 18), at 158.

22 For example, Hodgson proposed island size as a "reasonable basis for differentiation" and categorised islands as "rocks .001 (sq. miles in area), "islets" (.001–1 sq. miles), "isles" (1–1,000 sq. miles) and "islands" (over 1,000 sq. miles). See, R Hodgson, *Islands: Normal and Special Circumstances*, (U.S. Department of State, Bureau of Intelligence and Research, Research Study: Washington D.C., 1973), at 17.

23 As suggested by the United Kingdom during the eleventh session of UNCLOS III but strongly opposed by Turkey among others. Prescott and Schofield (n 17), at 70.

24 Nandan and Rosenne (n 16), at 330–336; Beckman and Schofield (n 17), at 10; and, Franckx (n 18), at 159.

Article 121
Regime of islands

1. An island is a naturally formed area of land, surrounded by water, which is above water at high tide.
2. Except as provided for in paragraph 3, the territorial sea, the contiguous zone, the exclusive economic zone and the continental shelf of an island are determined in accordance with the provisions of this Convention applicable to other land territory.
3. Rocks which cannot sustain human habitation or economic life of their own shall have no exclusive economic zone or continental shelf.

The issue of distinguishing between types of insular features, especially what constitutes an "island" capable of extended maritime claims (EEZ and continental shelf) versus a "rock" which cannot generate such claims, is therefore of crucial significance. If an island deemed capable of generating EEZ and continental shelf claims had no maritime neighbours within 400 M, it could generate maritime jurisdictional claims encompassing 125,664 M^2 [431,014km^2] of territorial sea, EEZ and continental shelf rights.[25] In contrast, if a feature were deemed a mere "rock" incapable of generating EEZ and continental shelf rights, its maritime jurisdictional zone generative capacity is severely restricted to a territorial sea of 452 M^2 (1,550km^2) (see Figure 2).[26]

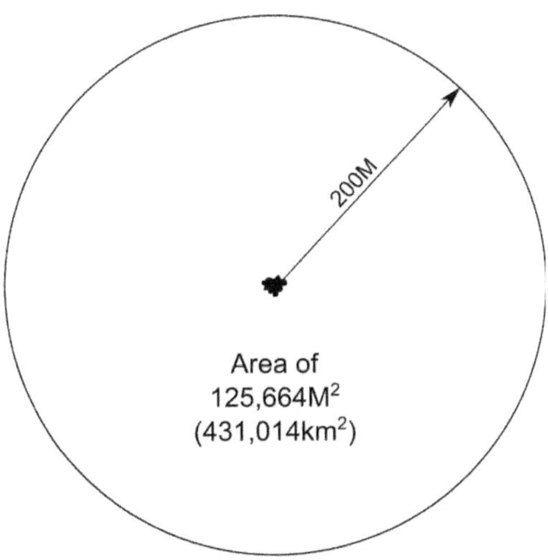

FIGURE 2
Maritime Entitlements of Islands and Rocks
SOURCE: PREPARED FOR THE AUTHOR BY I MADE ANDI ARSANA

25 Assuming for the purposes of this calculation the island in question is represented by a dot of no area. A "rock" within the meaning of Article 121(3) of the LOSC could also generate a contiguous zone to 24 M from baselines adding an additional 1,358 M^2. Calculations to the nearest M^2.

26 Prescott and Schofield (n 17), at 248–249.

2.3.1 Key Requirements for Insular Status

When the text of paragraph 1 of Article 121 is analysed in detail, it is clear that four key requirements for a feature to qualify legally as an island are identified: an island must be "naturally formed", be an "area of land", be "surrounded by water" and must also be "above water at high tide."

2.3.1.1 *Naturally Formed*

According to Anderson the term "naturally formed" means "created, maintained and shaped by the forces of nature."[27] This requirement clearly serves to disqualify artificial 'islands' such as platforms constructed for example on submerged shoals, low-tide elevations or reefs (see Section 4, below).

States have sought to preserve the insular status of certain naturally formed but unstable or erosion-threatened insular features through reclamation efforts. Alternatively, a vulnerable feature may either protected through the construction of hard coastal engineering measures such as sea walls and defences, designed to protect the insular feature through what has been termed a "bulkhead" policy or, in effect, 'built up' and potentially extended in area.[28]

A remarkable example of such an effort to preserve island status has been provided by Japan with respect to its southernmost island, Okinotorishima (Oki-no-Tori Shima).[29] Okinotorishima, while located on a broad reef platform, consists of two above high-tide features memorably described as "no larger than king-size beds",[30] which are marginally above the high-tide level.[31] Japan claims EEZ rights from these tiny features which, as Japan's southernmost territory, are important to parts of Japan's submission to the Commission on the Limits of the Continental Shelf (CLCS) concerning the outer limits of

---

27 Anderson (n 7), at 324.

28 D Freestone, 'International Law and Sea Level Rise' in RR Churchill and D Freestone (eds), *International Law and Global Climate Change* (Graham and Trotman/Martinus Nijhoff: London/Dordrecht, 1991), at 109–125 and 117–119; see also, D Freestone and CH Schofield, 'Options to Protect Coastlines and Secure Maritime Jurisdictional Claims in the Face of Global Sea Level Rise' in M Gerrard and G Wannier (eds), *Threatened Island Nations: Legal Implications of Rising Seas and a Changing Climate* (Cambridge University Press: Cambridge, 2013)141–165.

29 See, United Kingdom Hydrographic Office (UKHO) Admiralty Sailing Directions, *Pacific Islands Pilot*, NP60, Volume 1, 11th edition (Taunton: UKHO, 2007), at 467.

30 J Van Dyke, 'Speck in the Ocean Meets Law of the Sea', *New York Times*, Opinion, 21 January 1988, available at https://www.nytimes.com/1988/01/21/opinion/l-speck-in-the-ocean-meets-law-of-the-sea-406488.html.

31 The relevant British Admiralty Pilot refers to "a below-water reef" with the features on the reef are described as a "man-made islet, barely 10 cm above sea level". See, UKHO (n 29)' and, Prescott and Schofield (n 17), at 84–85.

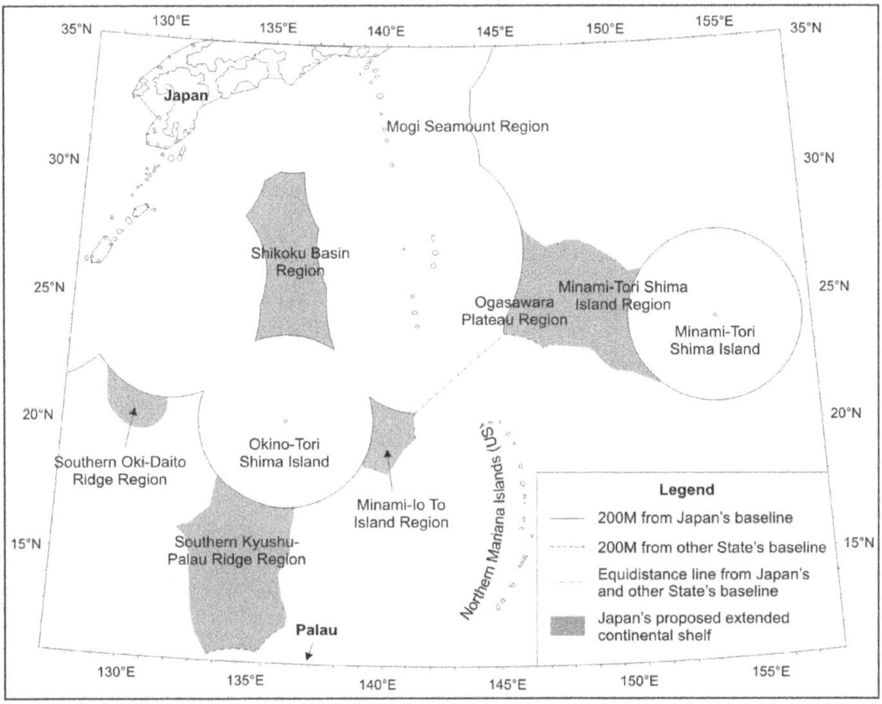

FIGURE 3 Japan's Maritime Claims in the vicinity of Okinotorishima
SOURCE: SCHOFIELD AND ARSANA[32]

its continental shelf seawards of 200 M, especially the Southern Kyushu-Palau Ridge Region (see Figure 3).[33]

The above high-tide features that make up Okinotorishima are vulnerable to erosion andin order to preserve the naturally above high-tide status, in the late 1980s Japan constructed sea defences, forming a 360 degree ring around each of the threatened features at a cost reported to be in excess of US$200 million.[34] These extensive maritime claims on the part of Japan

32 CH Schofield and IMA Arsana, 'Beyond the Limits?: Outer Continental Shelf Opportunities and Obligations in East and Southeast Asia', (2009) 31(1) *Contemporary Southeast Asia* 28–63, at 45. See also, Japan, 'Japan's Submission to the Commission on the Limits of the Continental Shelf, Executive Summary', 12 November 2008, available at http://www.un.org/Depts/los/clcs_new/submissions_files/submission_jpn.htm, at 6.

33 Ibid.

34 Brown *et al.*, writing in 1991, put the estimated cost of the project at £135 million. J Brown, A Colling, D Park, J Phillips, D Rothery and J Wright, *Case Studies in Oceanography and Marine Affairs* (Pergamon Press: Oxford, 1991), at 84–85; and, Prescott and Schofield (n 17), at 84–85. Silverstein, quoting Japanese sources, states that the three-year project, starting in 1988, was set to cost US$240 million. See, AL Silverstein, 'Okinotorishima: Artificial

in relation to Okinotorishima have been protested by neighbouring States, including China (see Section 3).[35]

As well as being costly to undertake, it is also now well-established that such hard coastal engineering can have unanticipated and unwelcome 'knock-on' impacts elsewhere along the coast. In particular, the construction of hard sea defences on one part of an island's coast may interrupt natural sediment flows, starving the supply of material elsewhere along the coast, leading to enhanced and unlooked for erosion.[36] Should such coastal protection measures lead to impacts crossing an international boundary, then transboundary international legal repercussions could arise.[37] These well-known drawbacks to hard coastal defences have led to the emergence of more ecosystem-based and environmentally sensitive 'soft engineering', 'ecological engineering' or 'green infrastructure' approaches aimed at delivering "coastal protection using natural systems".[38]

Preservation of a Speck of Sovereignty' (1990) 16(2) *Brooklyn Journal of International Law* 409–431, at 410. Additional construction work on facilities at Okinotorishima, costing ¥13 billion (over US$100 million), was reported in 2016. See, J Ryall, 'Japan spends millions building structures on uninhabited rocks 1,740 km from Tokyo to mark its territory', *South China Morning Post*, 2 February 2016, available at https://www.scmp.com/news/asia/east-asia/article/1908706/japan-spends-millions-building-structures-uninhabited-rocks-1740.

35 This is made clear through the diplomatic notes directed to the United Nations Secretary General made be these States in response to Japan's submission to the Commission on the Limits of the Continental Shelf (CLCS).See, https://www.un.org/Depts/los/clcs_new/submissions_files/submission_jpn.htm. These protests led to the Commission to decide not to provide recommendations for the Southern Kyushu-Palau Ridge Region. See, CLCS, 'Summary of Recommendations of the Commission on the Limits of the Continental Shelf in Regard to the Submission Made by Japan on 12 November 2008', 19 April 2012, at 4, available at https://www.un.org/Depts/los/clcs_new/submissions_files/jpn08/com_sumrec_jpn_fin.pdf.

36 D Freestone and J Pethick, 'Sea Level Rise and Maritime Boundaries: International implications of impacts and responses' in GH Blake (ed.), *International Boundaries: Fresh Perspectives*, Volume 5 (Routledge: London, 1994) 73–90 at 83–84; R Kenchington, 'Maintaining Coastal and Lagoonal Ecosystems and Productivity', in H Terashima (ed.) *Proceedings of The International Symposium of Islands and Oceans* (Ocean Policy Research Foundation: Tokyo, 2009) 1–11, at 4.

37 D Freestone and J Pethick, 'International Legal Implications of Coastal Adjustments Under Sea Level Rise: Active or Passive Policy Responses?' in UNEP/WMO/USACE/EPA/NOAA, Changing Climate and the Coast. Report to the Intergovernmental Panel on Climate Change from the Miami Conference on Adaptive Responses to Sea Level Rise and Other Impacts of Global Climate Change, Volume 1 (Environmental Protection Agency: Washington, 1990) 237–256, at 243–245. P Birnie, A Boyle and C Redgwell, *International Law and the Environment*, 3rd edition (Oxford University Press: Oxford, 2009), at 137.

38 See also, Freestone and Pethick (n 36), at 85.

2.3.1.2 *Area of Land*

The requirement that an island be composed of "an area of land" would seem, at first glance, to be self-evident. Anderson observes that this means "terra firma" and can be composed of a range of substances.[39] In certain circumstances, however, this seemingly straightforward aspect of insular definition can be problematic and open to dispute.[40]

Authoritative clarification on the issues of both area and composition of insular features was provided by the Nicaragua-Colombia case, on which the International Court of Justice (ICJ) rendered its Judgment in November 2012.[41] In this case, one of the parties to the dispute, Nicaragua, argued that a particular feature, designated as "QS32" located on a large bank called Quitasueño, did not qualify as a feature to which Article 121 of the LOSC applied because of it being composed of coral debris and its small size.

The Court dismissed both of these arguments.[42] With respect to the issue of "area of land" in particular, the Court stated in explicit terms that "the fact that the feature is composed of coral is irrelevant",[43] as:

> [i]nternational law defines an island by reference to whether it is "naturally formed" and whether it is above water at high tide, not by reference to its geological composition.[44]

This ruling on the part of the ICJ that Article 121 applied to a coral formation helped to underpin the Tribunal's view in the South China Sea case that the term "rock" need not have a restrictive, geological, character (see Section 3).

---

39 Anderson (n 7), at 324.

40 See, for example, the dispute between the Alaskan State authorities and the U.S. Federal Government concerning the status of Dinkum Sands which turned on whether this features, which includes sea ice, constituted "land" as well as whether that part of the formation's vertical height made up of ice could contribute to its elevation above high-tide. See, CR Symmons, *When is an 'Island' Not an 'Island' in International Law? The Riddle of Dinkum Sands in the Case of US v. Alaska*, Maritime Briefing, 2(6) (International Boundaries Research Unit: Durham, 1999). See also, Supreme Court of the United States (March 1996) No. 84 (Original) (*Report of the Special Master*).

41 *Territorial and Maritime Dispute (Nicaragua v Colombia)*, [2012] ICJ Reports 50, at 191–193, https://www.icj-cij.org/public/files/case-related/124/124-20121119-JUD-01-00-EN.pdf. [hereinafter, Nicaragua-Colombia case].

42 Ibid., paras 35–37.

43 Ibid., para. 37.

44 Ibid.

2.3.1.3 *Surrounded by Water*

The "surrounded by water" requirement may also be regarded as straightforward. If a feature is linked to the mainland coast by, for example, a sandbar, to such an extent that it may be considered an integral part of the mainland coast, then it follows that that feature takes on the characteristics of the mainland coast. As such, the feature would have a baseline and thus be capable of generating claims to the full suite of maritime zones, just as it would do as a fully-entitled island.

2.3.1.4 *Above High Tide*

A particular insular feature's relationship to the tidal level is vital in distinguishing between islands (above high-tide), low-tide elevations (above low-tide but submerged at high-tide) and non-insular features (submerged at low-tide) (see Figure 4). This classification will, in turn have an impact on the capacity of the feature in question to generate claims to maritime jurisdiction (see below).[45]

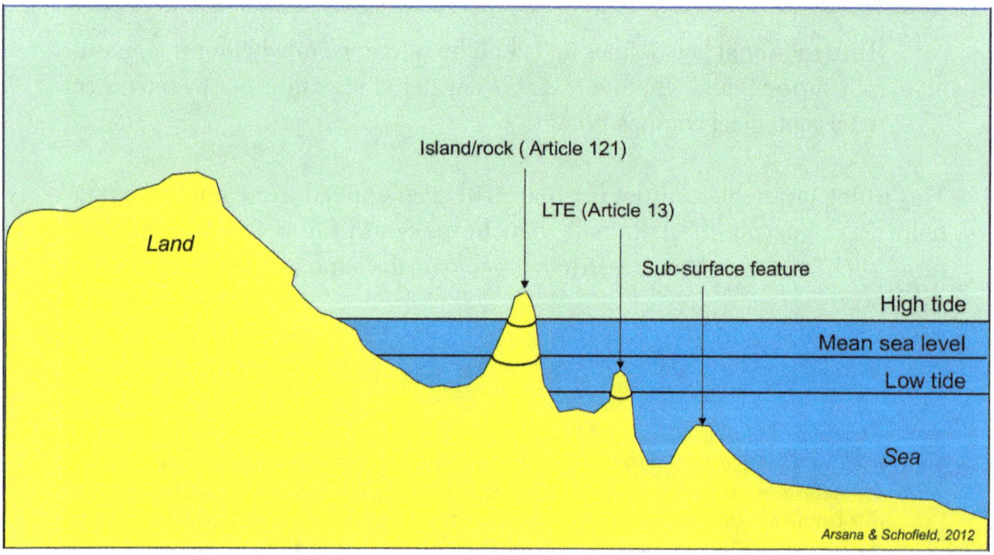

FIGURE 4 Insular Features and Sea Level
SOURCE: ARSANA AND SCHOFIELD, 2014[46]

45 CM Carleton and CH Schofield, *Developments in the Technical Determination of Maritime Space: Charts, Datums, Baselines, Maritime Zones and Limits*, Maritime Briefing, 3(3) (International Boundaries Research Unit, Durham: 2001), at 38.

46 IHO (n 5), Figure 4.3, Chapter 4, 9.

Whether a feature is above high-tide is directly linked to the choice of vertical datum used. That is, whether an insular feature is above the level of reference for vertical measurements such as depths and heights. Here it can be observed that while land survey systems generally use mean sea level (MSL) to define the height datum or reference level from which altitudes on land mapping are measured, hydrographic surveyors concerned generally use either a sampling or averages of high-waters derived from tide gauges in order to define the hydrographic shoreline shown on nautical charts. The Technical Aspects of the Law of the Sea (TALOS) Manual issued by the International Hydrographic Organization (IHO), notes, with some understatement, that "the issue of vertical datums remains complex."[47] No universally accepted vertical tidal datum is in use, however – leaving the choice to the coastal State and thus providing potential scope for dispute.[48]

For example, in the above-mentioned Nicaragua-Colombia case,[49] the parties disagreed over the tidal model that should be used to determine highest astronomical tide (HAT) – Colombia preferred the global Grenoble Tide Model while Nicaragua argued in favour of the Admiralty Total Tide model produced by the United Kingdom Hydrographic Office (UKHO).[50]

This was a critical consideration with respect to the status of Quitasueño, a large shoal or bank approximately 57 km long and 20 km wide. Colombia relied on two surveys,[51] which identified 34 features on Quitasueño that in its view qualified as islands by virtue of them being above high-tide as well as a further 20 features which qualified as low-tide elevations located within 12 M of one or more of the above high-tide features and so qualified as potential basepoints for measuring maritime entitlements (see Section 4, below). These features were designated QS1–54.[52]

47 Ibid., Chapter 2, at 16. This being because tidal levels are influenced by the phases of the Moon, the elliptical orbits of the Sun and the Moon, the Moon's changing declination as well as coastal configuration and physiography meaning that a global, universally applicable vertical datum remains out of reach. Ibid., Chapter 2, at 18–19.

48 Ibid., at 21–25. See also, Anderson (n 7), at 324; and, NSM Antunes, *The importance of the tidal datum in the definition of maritime limits and boundaries*, Maritime Briefing, 2(7) (International Boundaries Research Unit: Durham, 2000).

49 Nicaragua-Colombia case (n 41).

50 Ibid., para. 30.

51 Namely, a 'Study on Quitasueño and Alburquerque' prepared by the Colombian Navy in September 2008 and the Expert Report by Dr Robert Smith. See, R Smith, 'Mapping the Islands of Quitasueño (Colombia) – Their Baselines, Territorial Sea, and Contiguous Zone' of February 2010. See, Nicaragua-Colombia case (n 41), para. 29.

52 Nicaragua-Colombia case (n 41), para. 29.

In contrast, Nicaragua took the view that all of the features on Quitasueño are permanently submerged at high-tide.[53] Nicaragua argued that it was "inappropriate" to use the global Grenoble Tide Model to determine which features were above HAT as such global models as "quite inaccurate" in shallow waters, such as those around Quitasueño, and thus "unsuitable for navigation and other practical applications".[54] . Columbia countered these criticisms on the grounds that "international law does not prescribe the use of any particular method of tidal measurement", that the measurements of the many features made by its technical expert, Dr Robert Smith, were "accurate and clear", and that his approach to whether those features were above water at "high tide" was "conservative", because it was "based upon HAT rather than mean high tide."[55]

Ultimately, the Court did not indicate a preferred vertical datum for the determination of high-tide because one of the features on Quitasueño, "QS32", was above high-tide for either of the high-tide option proposed by the parties.[56] The Court also referred back to the Qatar-Bahrain case before the ICJ where the tiny feature Qit'at Jaradah was determined to be an island "notwithstanding that it is only 0.4 metres above water at high tide".[57] Regarding the other features very close to the high-tide level, the Court took a conservative view and determined that their insular status had not been conclusively proven.[58]

Vertical datum issues are also critical with respect to determining low-water lines which provide the normal baselines of islands which meet the requirements of Article 121(1) of the LOSC, consistent with Article 5 of the LOSC and in common with other above high-tide territory.[59] This provides that, save where otherwise provided in the Convention, a coastal State's normal baselines comprise "the low-water line along the coast as marked on large-scale charts officially recognized by the coastal State".[60] Baselines along the coast are

---

53 Ibid., para. 28.

54 This was the view expressed in a United States National Aeronautics and Space Administration (NASA) publication concerning global tidal models. See ibid., para. 30.

55 Ibid., para. 30.

56 QS 32 was determined to be 1.2m above high-tide using the Grenoble Tide Model as a basis for assessment and 0.7m above high-tide if the Admiralty Total Tide model was applied. Ibid., para. 37.

57 Ibid., para. 37. See also, Case Concerning Maritime Delimitation and Territorial Questions between Qatar and Bahrain (Qatar v. Bahrain) (Merits) [2001] ICJ Reports 40, para. 197 (hereinafter the Qatar-Bahrain case).

58 Nicaragua-Colombia case (n 41), para. 38.

59 See, Anderson (n 7), at 326.

60 LOSC, Article 5. This is a near verbatim repetition of Article 3 of the 1958 Convention on the Territorial Sea and Contiguous Zone.

significant in law of the sea terms because they provide the 'starting line' for the measurement of the limits of maritime claims and are also frequently critically important in the delimitation of maritime boundaries as a consequence of their direct role in the construction of equidistance lines.[61]

It can also be noted that Islands also play a significant role with respect to other types of baselines provided for under the LOSC, namely reefs (Article 6),[62] straight baselines (Article 7),[63] bays (Article 10)[64] and archipelagic baselines (Article 47).[65] However, these straight line types of baselines remain at least partially dependent on the location of normal baselines as they rely on turning points located on the low-water line.[66]

Analogous to the above high-tide requirement contained in Article 121(1), Article 5 is silent as to which vertical datum, and thus which among the many possible low-water lines that intersect the coast, is to be utilized. The issue is

---

61 See, also, See, Prescott and Schofield (n 17), at 239–240; and, CH Schofield, 'Defining the "Boundary" between Land and Sea: Territorial Sea Baselines in the South China Sea', in R Beckman, MR Page and L Bernard (eds), *UNCLOS and the South China Sea* (Edward Elgar Publishers: Cheltenham, 2014) 21–54.

62 With respect to reefs, Article 6 of the LOSC refers to "islands situated on atolls or of islands having fringing reefs", meaning that there is a clear for an island in keeping with Article 121(1) to be located on the reef in question. See, LOSC, Article 6. See also, Schofield (n 61), at 26.

63 Article 7(1) provides that straight baselines may be defined where "a fringe of islands along the coast in its immediate vicinity" exists. LOSC is, however, silent as to how many islands are required to form a fringe, how close to one another they need to be or, indeed, how far offshore they can be to meet the "immediate vicinity of the coast" requirement. See, for example, Prescott and Schofield (n 17), at 147; United Nations, *Baselines: An Examination of the Relevant Provisions of the United Nations Convention on the Law of the Sea* (United Nations, Office for Ocean Affairs and the Law of the Sea: New York, 1989), at 20–21; United States Department of State, *Developing Standard Guidelines for Evaluating Straight Baselines*, Limits in the Seas, No.106 (Bureau of Oceans and International Environmental and Scientific Affairs: Washington D.C., 31 August 1987); and CG Lathrop, JA Roach and DR Rothwell (eds), "Baselines under the International Law of the Sea: Reports of the International Law Association (ILA) Committee on Baselines under the International Law of the Sea" (2019) 2(1–2) *Brill Research Perspectives on the Law of the Sea*, at 66–82.

64 Article 10(3) addresses the issue of the presence of islands in the mouth of a bay such that the bay has several entrances by providing, with respect to the application of the semi-circle test at Article 10(2), that "the semi-circle shall be drawn on a line as long as the sum total of the lengths of the lines across the different mouths." See, LOSC, Article 10.

65 Islands are clearly fundamental to both to archipelagic status and defining archipelagic baselines. See, Articles 46–47 of the LOSC. See, Prescott and Schofield (n 17), at 168–178; and, Lathrop *et al.* (n 63), at 98–112 and 121.

66 United Nations (n 63), at 23.

therefore left to the discretion of coastal States.[67] That said, chart makers, with safety of navigation considerations foremost in mind, have tended to use a conservative chart datum and thus low water level which will be rarely reached.[68] A particularly conservative option, taking into account observations over at least 19 years in order to take into account the above-mentioned astronomical variations, is lowest astronomical tide (LAT) as used on many, though not all, nautical charts.[69]

With respect to vertical datum issues the Tribunal in the South China Sea case noted the existence of several "common datums" for measuring high water including Mean High Water,[70] Mean Higher High Water[71] and Mean High Water Springs.[72] It has been noted that these different measures of high water are by no means the same.[73] However, the Tribunal took the view that it neither the LOSC nor customary international law mandated "that the status of low-tide elevations and high-tide features/islands be determined against any particular high-water datum."[74]

Accordingly, the Tribunal considered that "States are free under the Convention to claim a high-tide feature or island on the basis of any high-water datum that reasonably corresponds to the ordinary meaning of the term 'high tide'" appearing in Articles 13 and 121 of the LOSC.[75] Having observed that ordinarily the height datum used on nautical charts of the coastal State concerned would be used, the Tribunal rather dryly commented that this was

67 See, Carleton and Schofield (n 45), at 21–25.

68 As Beazley observed, while there is "no agreed tidal level to which all chart datums conform", nonetheless there is international agreement that the vertical datum used for charting purposes should be "at a plane so low that the tide will not frequently fall below it." P Beazley, *Technical Aspects of Maritime Boundary Delimitation,* Maritime Briefing, 1(2) (International Boundaries Research Unit: Durham, 1994), at 6. See also, IHO (n 5), Chapter 2, at 16–21.

69 LAT is defined as: "the lowest level that can be predicted to occur under average meteorological conditions and under a combination of astronomical conditions". See, ibid., Chapter 2, at 19.

70 Defined as the average height of all high waters at a place over a 19-year period. South China Sea Arbitration, Award, (n 3), para. 310.

71 Defined as the average height of higher high water at a place over a 19-year period. Ibid.

72 Defined as the average height of the high waters of spring tides. Ibid.

73 See, Y Lyons, LQ Hung and P Tkalich, 'Determining high-tide features (or islands) in the South China Sea under Article 121(1): a legal and oceanography perspective', in S Jayakumar, et al (n 18), 128–153, at 135.

74 Ibid., para. 311.

75 Ibid.

"complicated" by the fact that the insular features of the South China Sea under consideration were claimed by "multiple States".[76]

The Tribunal took into consideration the height datums used by the parties to the case. That is the Philippines use of Mean High Water on its modern charting as compared to China's 1985 National Vertical Datum of China corresponding to Mean Sea Level as observed at Qingdao on the Yellow Sea.[77] The latter option was dismissed by the Tribunal on the grounds that it was of "no assistance" in determining the appropriate high-tide level to apply to insular status, though it was noted that on Chinese charts rocks and islets are depicted if they exceed Mean High Water Springs in elevation.[78]

Concerning tidal issues, the Tribunal took note of the present author's statement in his independent expert report (with the late Professor Victor Prescott and Mr Robert Van de Poll) to the Tribunal that:

> ... defining tidal levels is likely to be technically challenging in the context of the complex tidal regime of the South China Sea which is variable spatially and temporally and which has not been subject to detailed hydrographic surveys in recent times.[79]

Indeed, the Tribunal acknowledged the limitations of the hydrographic evidence before it noting that the "majority of the nautical charts of the South China Sea issued by different States, however, are to a greater or lesser extent copies of one another" and that there is a distinct "paucity of large-scale charting", something that was attributed to the "remoteness of many of the reefs, the limited amount of detailed survey work in the area".[80] Consequently, the Tribunal considered that the consistent depiction of features on successive charts to be insufficient evidence to make a "sensitive determination".[81]

Nonetheless, on the basis of historical observations of tidal levels and surveys including those of the navies of the United Kingdom, Japan and China, the Tribunal was "comfortable" that it had sufficient understanding of the average tidal range in the Spratly Islands to enable it to interpret charts and survey

---

76 Ibid., paras 311–312. See also discussion on this issue in Lyons et al (n 73), at 138–141.

77 Ibid., para. 313.

78 Ibid.

79 CH Schofield, JRV Prescott and R van der Poll, *An Appraisal of the Geographical Characteristics and Status of Certain Insular Features in the South China Sea* (March 2015), at 7. South China Sea Arbitration, Award (n 3), para. 317.

80 South China Sea Arbitration, Award, (n 3), para. 330.

81 Ibid., para. 331.

data, but that in its view it was not "feasible to predict with sufficient certainty the exact tidal state at a particular feature at any precise point in time."[82]

This conclusion had implications for the satellite imagery evidence presented by the Philippines which was considered to be "helpful" but suffered from the key shortcoming of the time of image capture not aligning with high or low tide.[83]

Here it is intriguing that the Tribunal's emphasis on historical hydrographic material was in distinct contrast with the approach of the ICJ in the only international case addressing the issue of tide levels and insular status, the Nicaragua-Colombia case.[84] In that case the Court did not regard "surveys conducted many years (in some cases many decades) before the present proceedings" to be "relevant" to the issue of determining whether or not naturally formed areas of land above high-tide existed on the feature Quitasueño.[85] Nor did the ICJ see "much probative value" in the charts relied on by Nicaragua although the reasoning for this was puzzling – that the charts were prepared to "show dangers to shipping" rather than to show "features which are just above, and those which are just below, water at high tide",[86] even though this is precisely what is depicted on nautical charts. Instead, the Court opted to reply on "contemporary evidence" including the above-mentioned Smith Report as this was based on "actual observations of conditions" combined with their "scientific evaluation."[87]

Although the approaches of the South China Sea Arbitral Tribunal and the ICJ differed from one another, this "discretion in the assessment of facts" has been viewed as being in keeping with the "prerogative essential to judges" in reaching their decisions.[88] As the South China Sea Tribunal noted the ICJ's concerns over the probative value of historical surveys but took the view that

82 Ibid., para. 319.

83 Ibid., para. 323. On the use of geospatial intelligence or "GEOINT" in the form of satellite and airborne imagery, nautical charts and sailing directions by the Tribunal see, SG Keating, 'Rock of Island? It Was an UNCLOS Call: The Legal Consequence of Geospatial Intelligence to the 2016 South China Sea Arbitration and the Law of the Sea' (2018) 9 *Journal of National Security Law & Policy* 509–547, at 534–537 (emphasis in original).

84 Nicaragua-Colombia case (n 41).

85 See, ibid., para. 35. On this point Murphy suggests that this was "presumably because the height of the features can vary over time." See also SD Murphy, *International Law relating to Islands*, Pocketbooks of The Hague Academy of International Law (Brill/Nijhoff: The Hague, 2017), at 53.

86 See, Nicaragua-Colombia case (n 41), para. 35.

87 Ibid., para. 36.

88 Lyons et al. (n 73) at 132.

these issues "must be understood in the context of that case".[89] Instead, the Tribunal noted that sailing directions provide an alternative source of direct observations, independently sought "original survey data" and benefitted from the assistance of an expert hydrographer in making its determinations.[90]

The fundamental reason for these contrasting approaches lies in the fact that large-scale reclamation and island-building efforts in the South China Sea context meant that the physical characteristics of features had been comprehensively transformed, undermining the value of contemporary observations which, in any case, were not possible,[91] leading the Tribunal to use "the best evidence available to it and drawing heavily on historical sources."[92]

Consequently, although the Tribunal indicated a preference for the most recent available evidence,[93] with respect to historical hydrographic information such as charts, records of surveys and sailing directions, the Tribunal in the South China Sea case observed that certain features such as rocks and large coral boulders cemented to the reef platform "have a high degree of permanence", even over centennial time-scales and that "[o]lder direct observations are thus not *per se* less valuable, provided they are clear in content and obtained from a reliable source."[94]

Of particular note in this context is that coasts, including those of islands, are well established to be dynamic features of the land/seascape that change or fluctuate in location over time.[95] As normal baselines are coincident with the low-water line, this means that as coastlines and low-water lines move or "ambulate" over time, so the maritime jurisdictional limits measured from them will necessarily also shift and change.[96] Consequently, some insular features, especially ones of low-elevation insular and composed of soft sandy or silty substances, may be ephemeral in character, appearing above high-tide

---

89 Ibid.

90 Ibid., paras 317 and 331–332.

91 Ibid., para. 327.

92 Ibid., para. 1179.

93 For example, with respect to assessing McKennan Reef when faced with older British and Japanese sources as opposed to a more recent Chinese chart, the Chinese was "preferred as the more recent evidence". See, South China Sea Arbitration, Award (n 3), para. 354. See also, Murphy (n 85), at 54.

94 South China Sea Arbitration, Award (n 3), para. 327. See also, Murphy (n 85), at 54–55.

95 See, W Hirst and D Robertson, 'Geographic information systems, charts and UNCLOS: Can they live together?', *Maritime Studies* 136 (May-June 2004) 1–6.

96 MW Reed, *Shore and Sea Boundaries: The Development of International Maritime Boundary Principles through United States Practice*, Volume 3 (U.S. Department of Commerce, National Oceanic and Atmospheric Administration, Washington: DC, 2000), at 185. See also, Lathrop, et al., 57–58.

and then disappearing below that level over time as the balance between depositional and erosive forces shifts. Traditionally, such changes have taken place as a result of natural depositional or erosional processes.[97] However, as a result of anthropogenically-induced significant and accelerating global sea level rise,[98] the prospect of the potential inundation and retreat of coasts, including the complete submergence or disappearance of low-elevation islands, has been raised.[99]

Although the Tribunal acknowledged that more "ephemeral features" such as sand cays "pose a greater challenge", it was also noted that they can also be "consistent over time", reforming in the same location, for instance if "dispersed by a storm."[100] Indeed, the Tribunal appears to have been comfortable with insular features being impermanent in character, taking the view that, "it is possible that a sand cay may be dispersed by storm action and reform in the same location after a short while", leading to the view that "The absence of a sand cay at a particular point in time is thus not conclusive evidence of the absence of a high-tide feature" with the Tribunal preferring historical evidence of the presence of the feature.[101] This finding has been challenged on the grounds that this reliance on historical evidence of up to 154 years vintage does not take into account sea level rise of at least 20 cm.[102] It has also been noted that the Tribunal's

97 For example, deposition from rivers advancing deltas seaward, the incremental advance of coastlines as a result of isostatic (or post-glacial) rebound whereby the continental crust is gradually rising following the removal of the enormous weight of major ice-sheets, some several kilometres thick, with the onset of the present inter-glacial period as well as uplift as a result of tectonic or volcanic activity.

98 The Intergovernmental Panel on Climate Change (IPCC) has been explicit in stating that sea level rise currently being experienced is "unprecedented over the last century" and that global mean sea level rise in the period 2006–2015 has been two and a half times the rate for the period 1901–1990. See, IPCC, 'Special Report on the Ocean and Cryosphere in a Changing Climate', approved at its 51st Session, 20–23 September 2019, at 10, available at https://www.ipcc.ch/srocc/home/.

99 See, for example, D Vidas, D Freestone and J McAdam (eds), 'International Law and Sea Level Rise: Report of the International Law Association Committee on International Law and Sea Level Rise' (2019) 2(3) *Brill Research Perspectives on the Law of the* Sea; CH Schofield, 'Climate Change and Changing Coasts: Geophysical and Jurisdictional Implications of Sea Level Rise' (2017) 5(1) *Korean Journal of International and Comparative Law* 36–60. See also, CH Schofield and D Freestone, 'Islands Awash Amidst Rising Seas?: Sea Level Rise and Insular Status under the Law of the Sea' (2019) 34 *International Journal of Marine and Coastal Law* 391–414.

100 South China Sea Arbitration, Award (n 3), para. 327.

101 Ibid., para. 373.

102 Lyons et al. (n 73) at 133, where global mean sea level rise over the period was conservatively suggested to be "at least 20 cm". See also, Keating (n 83) at 544.

apparent assumption that such sediment and sandy features in the South China Sea reform in the same location may be misplaced as they can be transient in character, forming and reforming intermittently and in different locations as well as shapes and sizes.[103]

2.3.2 Rocks

Rocks are a category of island, since they are defined as part of Article 121 dealing with the regime of islands,[104] but can be thought of as a disadvantaged sub-category of islands whose zone-generative capacity, and thus value to a potential claimant, is significantly reduced. For its part the South China Sea Arbitral Tribunal distinguished between "the two categories of naturally formed above high tide insular features" covered by Article 121 of the LOSC as "fully entitled islands" and "rocks".[105] It is important to note that in order to qualify as a rock, the other requirements for insular status laid down elsewhere in Article 121 must first be met, notably the conditions laid out in paragraph 1 of Article 121 as outlined above.

As previously noted, if an island deemed capable of generating EEZ and continental shelf claims had no maritime neighbours within 400 M, it could generate enormous maritime jurisdictional claims as compared with a mere "rock" unable to do so. This crucial distinction was explored in detail in the South China Sea case (see Section 3).

2.4 *Progress towards the Clarification of the Regime of Islands*

Beyond examination of the drafting history of Article 121 of the LOSC, a number of potential sources of clarification of the regime of islands exist. The practice of States in their interpretation and application of Article 121 of the LOSC may provide one such source of clarity regarding the provisions concerned.

103 Ibid., at 144–146. On the issue of whether a feature needs to be permanently above a particular water level or can be occasionally overtopped see, Anderson (n 7), at 324; CR Symmons, *The Maritime Zones of Islands in International Law* (Martinus Nijhoff: The Hague, 1979), at 10–11 and 42–43; CR Symmons, *Some Problems Relating to the Definition of Insular Features in International Law*, Maritime Briefing, 1(5) (International Boundaries Research Unit: Durham, 1995), at 25–26; and, PB Beazley, *Maritime limits and baselines: A guide to their delineation*, (3rd ed, The Hydrographic Society, Special Publication No.2, 1987).

104 The South China Sea Arbitral Tribunal was explicit on this point stating that "Within Article 121, rocks are a category of island." See, South China Sea Arbitration, Award (n 3), para. 481.

105 Ibid., para. 390.

International courts and tribunals may also play an important role in such clarification. Further, the views of publicists may be of relevance.[106]

2.4.1 State Practice

Perhaps unsurprisingly, almost all coastal States have interpreted Article 121 in such a way that their own insular features are considered to be fully-entitled islands capable of generating an EEZ and a continental shelf. That is, with few exceptions, States in possession of insular features have tended to assert broad, maximalist claims to maritime jurisdiction, regardless of the remote, desolate and minimal or uninhabited nature of the insular features concerned which appear to possess little evidence of economic activity associated with them. This is well illustrated by Japan's above-mentioned maritime claims from Okinotorishima, though Japan is by no means alone in advancing such expansive maritime claims from insular features whose capacity for human habitation or an economic life of their own is questionable (see Figure 3).

There is, however, some contrary practice on the part of certain coastal States. For example, Mexico enacted legislation in 1986 which differentiates between types of island and indicating that while islands shall have an exclusive economic zone, "rocks that cannot sustain human habitation or economic life of their own shall not."[107] In practice all Mexican islands have been treated as fully entitled islands with the exception of Roca Alijos – a group of tiny (0.012 km^2), steep-to volcanic islets located in the Pacific Ocean approximately 162 M (300 km) west of Baja California on the Mexican mainland coast.[108]

The United Kingdom's treatment of Rockall, an isolated rocky pinnacle which lies approximately 163 M off the north-western coast of Scotland is also

106 VCLT (n 15), Article 31. See also Article 38(1)(d) of the Statute of ICJ which indicated that in deciding on disputes submitted to it in accordance with international law the Court shall apply, in addition to international conventions, international custom and general principles of international law "judicial decisions and teachings of the most highly qualifies publicists of the various nations, as subsidiary means for the determination of the rules of law." See, ICJ, Statute of the International Court of Justice, available at https://www.icj-cij.org/en/statute.

107 Mexico, Federal Act relating to the Sea, 8 January 1986, Article 51, available at http://www.un.org/Depts/los/LEGISLATIONANDTREATIES/PDFFILES/MEX_1986_Act.pdf.

108 See, Symmons, (n 103, 1979), at 125–126; and, AG Oude Elferink, 'Clarifying Article 121 (3) of the Law of the Sea Convention: the limits set by the nature of international legal processes' (1998) 6(2) *Boundary and Security Bulletin*, 58–68, at 59.

instructive.[109] Rockall is undoubtedly tiny,[110] such that, the leader of the first authenticated landing on Rockall, Captain Basil Hall, noted that "the smallest point of a pencil could scarcely give it a place on any map which would not exaggerate its proportions."[111] Although sovereignty over the feature is uncontested,[112] the United Kingdom's use of Rockall as a basepoint for defining its 200 M fishery zone limit in 1977 raised protests from the Kingdom of Denmark (on behalf of the Faeroe Islands) and Ireland.[113]

As a prelude to its accession to LOSC in 1997, however, the United Kingdom declared that Rockall was in fact a rock in line with Article 121(3) and thus was "not a valid basepoint for such limits."[114] This reclassification of Rockall as a "rock" within the meaning of Article 121(3) resulted in a 'roll back' and contraction in UK's fishery zone of around 60,000 square nautical miles (see Figure 5).[115] This change accords the fact that Rockall was cited as an example of a "rock" in the course of UNCLOS III, which resulted in LOSC, including, of course, Article 121.[116] It can also be noted that the United Kingdom does not claim a 200 M EEZ or continental shelf rights from Shag Rocks, a group of six small features located approximately 150 M northwest of the main island of South Georgia in the South Atlantic although Argentina which terms them Islas Aurora and also claims sovereignty over them does do so.[117]

---

109 See, F MacDonald, 'The Last Outpost of Empire: Rockall and the Cold War' (2006) 32 *The Journal of Historical Geography* 627–647, at 627–628.

110 MacDonald reports the area of Rockall as 784.3m² (Ibid.: 627). Oude Elferink suggests the figure of 642m². See Oude Elferink (n 108), at 59.

111 Quoted in MacDonald, (n 109), at 631.

112 The UK annexed Rockall on 17 September 1955. See, MacDonald (n 109) at, 634–635; and, ED Brown, 'Rockall and the Limits of National Jurisdiction of the UK' (1978) 2 *Marine Policy* 181–211.

113 Symmons (n 103, 1979), at 117–118.

114 House of Commons (HC) *Hansard, Written Answers*, 21 July 1997, cols. 397–398. An identical statement was made in the House of Lords a day later on July 22, 1997 (*Hansard* (HL) *Written Answers*, 22 July 1997, cols. 155–156. Quoted in DH Anderson, 'British Accession to the UN Convention on the Law of the Sea' (1997) 46 *International and Comparative Law Quarterly*, 761–786, at 778. See also, Oude Elferink (n 108), at 59.

115 Oude Elferink (n 108), at 78–93.

116 Anderson (n 114, at 778) writes that "Rockall was cited (in the hearing of the present writer) during the Third Conference on the Law of the Sea as an example of such a rock."

117 These contrasting claims are highlighted on a map provided by the International Boundaries Research Unit (IBRU). See, IBRU, 'Claims and potential claims to maritime jurisdiction in the South Atlantic and Southern Oceans by Argentina and the UK', available at https://www.dur.ac.uk/resources/ibru/south_atlantic_maritime_claims.pdf.

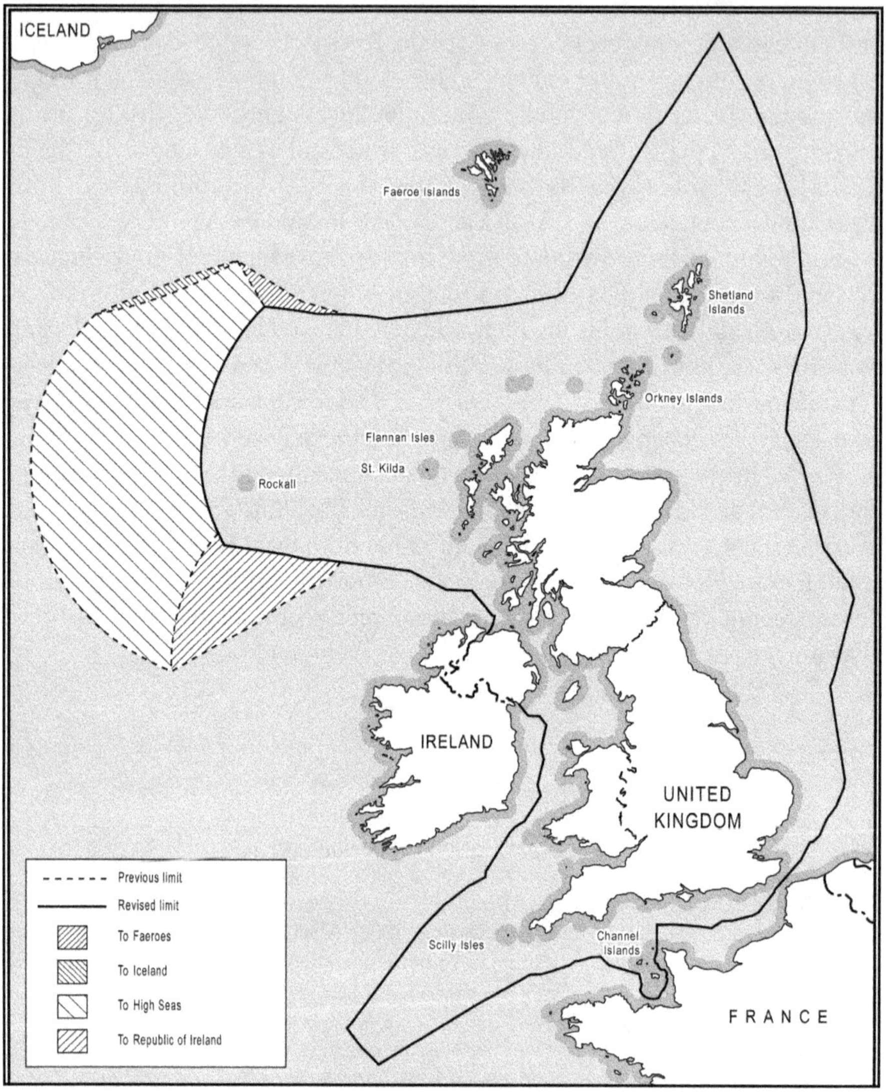

FIGURE 5 The United Kingdom's Rockall 'Roll-back'
SOURCE: IBRU, DURHAM UNIVERSITY, UK.[118]

118 Carleton and Schofield (n 45), at 59. See also, CR Symmons, 'Ireland and the Rockall Dispute: An Analysis of Recent Developments', *Boundary and Security Bulletin* (1998) 6(1), 78–93 at 85.

Additionally, in the context of maritime boundary delimitation numerous islands have been awarded only partial effect on the course of the boundary line or have been entirely ignored, especially where to accord these features full weight would result in disproportionate and thus inequitable impacts in the application of equidistance line-based maritime boundaries (see Section VI(A) below).[119]

2.4.2 Treatment of Islands in Judicial Decisions

International jurisprudence dealing with the definition or status of islands is relatively sparse. In contrast, international courts and tribunals have rendered numerous international decisions the treatment of islands in maritime delimitation. In this context islands have often been accorded a reduced effect on the course of maritime boundary lines. However, these cases have, naturally enough, focused on the delimitation of a line rather than on the status of particular insular features that may influence the course of such a delimitation line. Thus, while many islands have had no more influence on the delimitation line beyond 12 M, and have thus been *treated* as Article 121(3) rocks, the international judicial decisions in question are silent on the *status* of features.

In some cases this has been because the parties themselves were in agreement over the status of the insular features concerned or the maritime zones they can generate, obviating the need for the judicial body to assess their status, as occurred in the Jan Mayen[120] and Nicaragua-Honduras cases.[121] However, even when the parties to a delimitation case have presented extensive arguments on the interpretation of Article 121, international courts and tribunals have proved reluctant to do so. For example, in the Black Sea case between Romania and Ukraine before the ICJ, despite the status of a key potential basepoint, Ukraine's Serpents' Island, being a significant issue of contention between the parties in pleadings, the Court was able to achieve that outcome

119 See, for example, CH Schofield, 'Islands or Rocks – Is that the real question?: The Treatment of Islands in the Delimitation of Maritime Boundaries' in MH Nordquist, JN Moore, AHA Soons, and H-S Kim (eds), *The Law of the Sea Convention: US Accession and Globalization* (Martinus Nijhoff: Leiden/Boston, 2012), 322–340, 333–334.

120 See, Case Concerning Maritime Delimitation in the Area between Greenland and Jan Mayen (Denmark v. Norway), [1993] ICJ Reports, 38, at para. 61 [hereinafter the Jan Mayen case].

121 See, Case Concerning Territorial and Maritime Dispute between Nicaragua and Honduras in the Caribbean Sea (Nicaragua v. Honduras), Judgment of 8 October 2007, ICJ Reports 659, at 77, para. 137 [hereinafter, the Nicaragua-Honduras case].

without the "need to consider whether Serpents' Island falls under paragraphs 2 or 3 of Article 121."[122]

Island status issues have also arisen in the context of cases concerning illegal fishing before the International Tribunal for the Law of the Sea (ITLOS), notably in the *Monte Confurco*[123] and *Volga* cases[124] before ITLOS. In particular, one ITLOS Judge, Judge Budislav Vukas, pronounced specifically on the issue of islands and LOSC, Article 121. In the former case Judge Vukas was of the view that France was not entitled to proclaim an EEZ adjacent to the "uninhabitable and uninhabited" Kerguelen Islands in the southern Indian Ocean,[125] despite their size, reported to collectively be 7,215 km^2.[126]

The views of Judge Vukas were more explicitly articulated in relation to the Volga case which concerned the prompt release of a Russian-flagged fishing vessel, that was apprehended in the vicinity of Australia's Heard Island and McDonald Island. The status of these islands was not central to the case, not least because the Russia did not challenge Australia's 200 M claim around them.[127] However, in his Declaration in the Volga case Judge Vukas dissociated himself from the Tribunal's statements and conclusions based on the EEZ claim around these islands.[128]

Judge Vukas reached this view "concerning the appropriation of vast areas of the ocean by some States which possess tiny uninhabited islands thousands of miles from their own coasts",[129] on the basis of his understanding of the

122 The Court also observed that Serpents' Island had had a 12 M territorial sea attributed to it under previous agreements between the parties to the case. See, Case Concerning Maritime Delimitation in the Black Sea (Romania v. Ukraine), Judgment of 3 February 2009, [2009] ICJ Reports 61, paras 187–188 (hereinafter the Black Sea Case).

123 *The 'Monte Confurco' case (Seychelles v France)* (Judgment) 2000 ITLOS Case No 6, Declaration of Judge Vukas, para. 122 (hereinafter the Monte Confurco case).

124 The "Volga" Case (Russian Federation v. Australia) (Prompt Release) (2002) ITLOS Case No. 11 (hereinafter the Volga case), Declaration of Vice-President Vukas.

125 Here Judge Vukas was quoting Captain Yves-Joseph de Kerguelen-Trémarec who discovered the Kerguelen Islands. See, the Monte Confurco case (n 123), Declaration of Judge Vukas.

126 See, Monte Confurco case (n 123), Declaration of Judge Vukas. See, WL Gullett and CH Schofield, 'Pushing the Limits of the Law of the Sea Convention: Australian and French Cooperative Surveillance and Enforcement in the Southern Ocean' (2007) 22(4) *International Journal of Marine and Coastal Law*, 545–583, at 563–565; and, WL Gullett, 'The South China Sea Arbitration's Contribution to the Concept of Juridical Islands' (2018) 47 *Questions of International Law* 5–38, at 8.

127 Australia proclaimed a 200 M Australian Fishing Zone (AFZ) in November 1979 and this extends off most of Australia's external territories, including Heard Island and McDonald Island. Gullett and Schofield (n 126), at 547.

128 The Volga case (n 124), Declaration of Vice-President Vukas, para. 2.

129 Ibid.

reasons for the establishment of the EEZ regime.[130] Judge Vukas noted that many coastal States "considered it just and equitable to secure for their coastal population some priority in the fisheries even beyond the outer limits of their territorial sea" and outlined how this was taken into consideration at the First and Second United Nations conferences on the Law of the Sea (UNCLOS I and II).[131] He further observed that how preferential rights for the coastal State in related to fishing in adjacent waters was "a concept crystallized as customary international law by reference to the Fisheries Jurisdiction case of 1974.[132]

Judge Vukas went on to link the adoption of the EEZ regime at UNCLOS III to the "insistence of developing coastal States that the preferential rights of their population be recognized in an area beyond their territorial waters", coming to the conclusion that "the protection of the economic interests of the coastal States, and in particular their population in the coastal areas" was "the essential factor" in the establishment of the EEZ regime.[133] Judge Vukas further supported his reasoning by reference to the main provisions of the EEZ, in particular the "basic rule" that the sovereign rights of coastal States in the EEZ are "for the purpose of exploring and exploiting, conserving and managing the natural resources, whether living or non-living"[134] and that "conservation and management measures undertaken for the maintenance of the living resources in the zone have to take into account, inter alia, 'the economic needs of coastal fishing communities'".[135]

On the basis that the rationale for allowing coastal States to claim EEZs was to support coastal populations dependent on coastal fisheries and thereby to protect the economic interests of the coastal States, Judge Vukas was of the view "that the establishment of exclusive economic zones around rocks and other small islands serves no useful purpose and that it is contrary to international law."[136]

The islands in question are undoubtedly remote and inhospitable in character. Heard Island is located in sub-Antarctic waters over 2,200 M southwest of Perth in Western Australia (McDonald Island lies 23 M further west and the

130 Ibid., paras 3–5.

131 Ibid., para. 3.

132 Ibid., para. 4. See also, Fisheries Jurisdiction case (United Kingdom v. Iceland), Merits, Judgment, I.C.J. Reports 1974, 23.

133 The Volga case (n 124), Declaration of Vice-President Vukas, para. 5.

134 Ibid., and LOSC, Article 56(1)(a).

135 The Volga case (n 124), Declaration of Vice-President Vukas, para. 5: and LOSC, Article 61(3).

136 The Volga case (n 124), Declaration of Vice-President Vukas, para. 10.

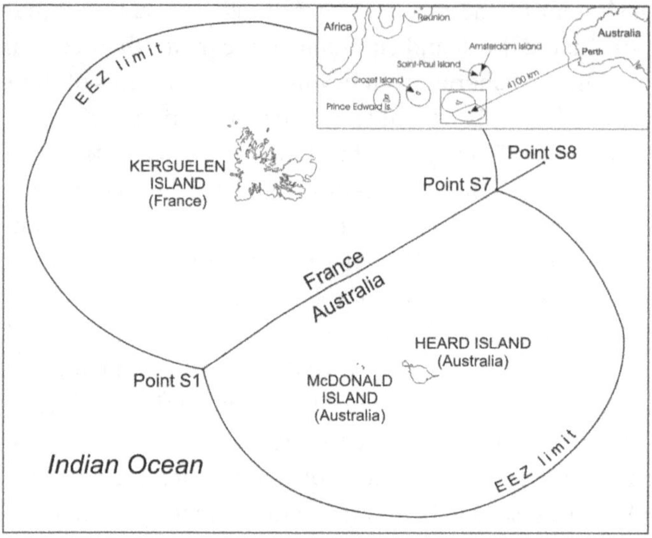

FIGURE 6 Heard Island and McDonald and Kerguelen Islands
SOURCE: GULLETT AND SCHOFIELD

Kerguelen group 238 M to the northwest).[137] They are by no means tiny features, however. While McDonald Island and its associated islets are around 2.5 km² in area, Heard Island covers an area of 368 km² and the Kerguelen archipelago encompasses 7,215 km² (Figure 6).[138] While Heard Island and McDonald Island lack permanent inhabitants, Kerguelen hosts a small settlement, largely devoted to supporting scientific research, which is manned year-round.[139]

Since the late 1990s Australia and France have, however, increased their efforts concerning the conservation and management of the fisheries resources in the waters around Heard Island and McDonald Island and the Kerguelen Islands. This occurred largely in response to a rise in illegal foreign

137 See Gullett and Schofield (n 126), at 548. See also, Geoscience Australia, 'Heard and McDonald Islands', available at https://www.ga.gov.au/scientific-topics/national-location-information/dimensions/remote-offshore-territories/heard-and-mcdonald-islands.

138 See, Australian Antarctic Division, 'About Heard Island', at http://www.heardisland.aq/about/location_geography.html; and, Ministère de l'Intérieur, de l'Outre-Mer et des Collectivitésterritoriales,'LesT.A.A.F.',availableathttp://www.outre-mer.gouv.fr/outremer/front?id=outremer/decouvrir_outre_mer/taaf/publi_P_les_t_a_a_f_1082040279389.

139 Heard Island has also supported sealers in the past. See also, Gullett and Schofield (n 126).

fishing, notably for the valuable Patagonian Toothfish[140] and has included legal, operational and cooperative dimensions.[141] Although Australia argued in the context of the Volga case that the establishment of the EEZ around Heard Island and McDonald Island "was useful for the more effective preservation of the marine resources" around those islands, Judge Vukas was unconvinced that these fisheries management efforts were enough to render them fully entitled islands.[142]

It can be observed in this context that Australia and France advanced claims to 200 M maritime zones since the late 1970s, they effectively recognised each other's EEZ claims from the islands in question through their maritime boundary delimitation of 1982.[143] These claims have also not resulted in any formal protest from other States. While, Judge Vukas's comments were issued through a separate declaration,[144] his intervention is highlighted here as it arguably illustrates judicial thinking on the regime of islands. Moreover, the reasoning he provided was to a large extent echoed by the South China Sea Tribunal, particularly in its interpretation of the context of Article 121(3) of the LOSC and the objective and purpose of the Convention (see Section 3.2.12, below).

2.4.3 Views of Commentators

Article 121 of the LOSC has proved to be a rich vein for scholarly effort among the law of the sea community over the years, with a view to clarifying the interpretation and application of its provisions. A number of these eminent scholars have reviewed the text of Article 121 of LOSC in detail and teased their way through the entrails of its drafting history with the objective of seeking guidance in the interpretation and application of Article 121, but to little avail.[145] Indeed, a review of the relevant literature reveals diverse and

---

140 There are two species of toothfish. The Antarctic toothfish (*Dissostichus mawsoni*) and the better-known Patagonian toothfish (*Dissostichus elegionides*) which is a demersal species otherwise known, especially in North America, as "Chilean Sea Bass".

141 See, Gullett and Schofield (n 126).

142 The Volga case (n 124), Declaration of Vice-President Vukas, para. 7.

143 See, Agreement on Marine Delimitation between the Government of Australia and the Government of the French Republic, 4 January 1982 (in force 10 January 1983). See also, Gullett and Schofield (n 126), at 547.

144 It may be that other ITLOS Judges took the view that this issue was not relevant to the issue of the prompt release of the fishing vessel which they were bound to consider without delay and therefore declined to comment one way or the other. See also, Gullett and Schofield (n 126), at 117.

145 A by no means exhaustive list of scholarly contributions on this issue includes, Brown (n 112); JI Charney, 'Rocks that cannot sustain human habitation' (1999) 93(4) *American*

contradictory interpretations of almost every term and phrase contained in Article 121 and indicates that no consensus on this issue has been reached. For example, while some commentators reached the view that the phrase "human habitation or economic life of their own" does not exclude islands obtaining external support, other writers disagreed, maintaining that the key test of the capacity of an island to sustain "human habitation or economic life of their own" is whether it can sustain, without external support and on the basis of its own natural resources, stable communities of organized groups of human beings.[146]

The aim here is not to re-tread the well-worn, if winding, paths of these debates. However, the views of Judge José Luis Jesus of the ITLOS,[147] albeit in his role as a publicist rather than as a Judge, are arguably worth highlighting as they to a large extent accord with those of the Tribunal in the South China Sea case. Writing in 2003,[148] he asserted in forthright terms that:

> The very purpose of the rock provision, as was intended by its proponents in the Law of the Sea conference and as crystallized in article 121, paragraph 3, was to deny tiny islands, referred to in the 1982 Convention as rocks, the capacity to generate unfairly and inequitably huge maritime spaces, on account of an EEZ or CS, which could, in most cases, impinge upon other States maritime space or on the area of the International Seabed, reserved for the Common Heritage of Mankind.[149]

It was further observed that this seems to have been a "fundamental objective" of the drafters of the LOSC "in order to restore a sense of balance to the

Journal of International Law 863–78.; Oude Elferink (n 108); B Kwiatkowska, and AHA Soons, 'Entitlement to maritime areas of rocks which cannot sustain human habitation or economic life of their own' (1990) XXI *Netherlands Yearbook of International Law* 139–81; Prescott and Schofield (n 17), at 61–75; JM Van Dyke and RA Brooks, 'Uninhabited islands: their impact on the ownership of the oceans' resources' (1983) 12 *Ocean Development International Law Journal* 265–84; JM Van Dyke, J Morgan and J Gurish, 'The exclusive economic zone of the northwestern Hawaiian Islands: when do uninhabited islands generate an EEZ?' (1988) 25(3) *San Diego Law Review* 425–494; and M Gjetnes, 'The Spratlys: Are they Rocks or Islands?' (2010) 32 *Ocean Development and International Law* 191–204.

146 See Van Dyke and Brooks (n 145), at 265–300; and, Charney (n 145), at 863–878.

147 Here it is important to note that Judge Jesus was writing in the role of a publicist rather than his capacity as a Judge and therefore his view would represent but a "subsidiary means for the determination of rules of law" in keeping with, for example, Article 38(1) (d) of the Statute of the ICJ. See ICJ (n 106).

148 JL Jesus, 'Rocks, New-born Islands, Sea Level Rise and Maritime Space', in J. Frowein *et al.* (eds) *Verhandeln für den Frieden: Negotiating for Peace, Liber amicorum Tonto Eitel* (Springer: Berlin, 2003) 579–603.

149 Ibid., at 588.

maritime space sharing provisions" of the Convention.[150] Jesus was rather acerbic in his view that the "human habitation" requirement under Article 121(3) "implies much more than the capacity to raise a tent".[151] However, if a feature were to be able sustain "without artificial additions all the activities and amenities that human habitation … normally implies" then it would be "equated with an island proper" with full maritime entitlements.[152] Otherwise, extending full island treatment to rocks would be "unfair and imbalanced".[153] He further commented that while no size criteria for rocks was included in Article 121(3) of the LOSC, nonetheless, the provision was included at least in part to address "cases where a rock's size would be so small that no meaningful habitation or economic life could possibly and naturally take place", in contrast to that on larger islands or mainland territory.[154]

With respect to the criteria of economic life Judge Jesus also noted that this accords with the idea of a feature "having the capacity or potentials of bearing an independent, though not necessarily self-sufficient economic life."[155] He further observed that the presence of a single resource of economic value would mean that "any rock however small and negligible" could meet the criterion and as it would always be possible to find something of economic value on the feature. Economic activities occurring in the waters around a feature were similarly rejected as it would be near to "impossible to find a rock, however small its size might be, that would not meet the economic life criterion" and that as such the provision "make no sense"[156] and that such an interpretation would "go beyond the drafters' clear intent."[157] Judge Jesus also noted with respect to the uncertainties in the interpretation of Article 121(3) of the LOSC:

> … since this compromise failed to consider which islands are to be seen as rocks and, among the rocks, which ones are to be considered as not capable of sustaining human habitation and an economic life of their own, the task of making this determination is left to doctrinal writings, judicial and arbitral decision, as well as to negotiations.[158]

150 Ibid.
151 Ibid.
152 Ibid., 589.
153 Ibid.
154 Ibid.
155 Ibid., at 590.
156 Ibid., at 591.
157 Ibid.
158 Ibid.

Overall, the key questions that arise in the interpretation and application of Article 121 outlined above defied ready interpretation based on the text of Article 121 together with its drafting history. Further, as noted above, State practice has been predominantly expansive in character. Moreover, while there is an abundance of both State practice and cases relating to the treatment of insular features in maritime boundary delimitation, both States and international courts and tribunals have largely been silent with respect to the status of particular insular features and have eschewed direct interpretation of Article 121. Substantial clarification of Article 121 has, however, emerged through the South China Sea case which for the first time saw an international judicial body squarely address the interpretation of the regime of islands under the LOSC.

3 The Regime of Islands Reframed: The South China Sea Award and Article 121

On 12 July 2016 the Arbitral Tribunal in in the case between the Philippines and China delivered its *Award*, following its earlier 29 October 2015 *Award on Jurisdiction and Admissibility*.[159] The Tribunal was therefore an ad hoc one, constituted under Annex VII of the LOSC, having been initiated by the Philippines.[160] The Permanent Court of Arbitration in The Hague acted as the registry for the case and venue for hearings, something which explains somewhat misleading references to it as the "PCA case" (see Section 5).

As both the Philippines and China are parties to LOSC they are subject to Part XV of the which deals with the settlement of disputes and which provides for "compulsory procedures entailing binding decisions".[161] It is these provisions that the Philippines invoked in order to bring the case. However, immediately subsequent articles of the Convention outline limitations and exceptions to the applicability of such binding dispute settlement provisions so as to exclude from consideration any unsettled disputes concerning "sovereignty or other rights over continental or insular land territory", "sea boundary

159 See, South China Sea Arbitration, Award and Award on Jurisdiction and Admissibility (n 3). The jurisdictional aspects of the case are not covered in the present study.

160 Philippines, 'Notification and Statement of Claim on the West Philippine Sea', 22 January 2013, available at http://www.pcacases.com/pcadocs/The%20Philippines%27%20Memorial%20-%20Volume%20III%20%28Annexes%201-60%29.pdf.

161 LOSC, Articles 286–296.

delimitations", or involving "historic bays or titles".[162] China activated these exceptions through a Declaration made on its ratification on 7 June 2006.[163]

The Philippines in its *Statement of Claim* was careful to frame its questions so as to avoid issues of sovereignty and maritime delimitation, instead raising issues which it contended arise from the interpretation and application of LOSC. However, China, for its part, returned the Philippines' notification of its claims, argued that the Tribunal lacked jurisdiction to hear the case,[164] and has rejected the Tribunal's Award.[165]

The Tribunal addressed these issues at considerable length in both its initial *Award on Jurisdiction and Admissibility* and the first part of its final *Award*.[166] Ultimately, the Tribunal was satisfied that, in keeping with its powers under the Convention, it had the necessary jurisdiction to address the vast majority of the issues and questions posed to it by the Philippines.[167] Moreover, under the Convention the Tribunal's Award is explicitly "final and binding and without appeal."[168]

It is worth noting here that the Tribunal went to considerable lengths to try to take China's views into consideration and not to simply rely on evidence

162 LOSC, Article 298(1)(a)(i).

163 See, United Nations Treaty Collection (UNTC), 'Status of Treaties: United Nations Convention on the Law of the Sea, Montego Bay, 10 December 1982', Declarations and Reservations, available at, https://treaties.un.org/Pages/ViewDetailsIII.aspx?src=TREATY&mtdsg_no=XXI-6&chapter=21&Temp=mtdsg3&clang=_en.

164 For example, in its "Position Paper" China argued that the disputes in question related to sovereignty and, if not that, then issues of maritime delimitation were implicated and that therefore the Tribunal lacked the jurisdiction to hear the case. See, China, 'Position Paper on the Matter of Jurisdiction in the South China Sea Arbitration Initiated by the Republic of the Philippines', 7 December 2014, available on the website of the Ministry of Foreign Affairs of China available at www.fmprc.gov.cn/nanhai/eng/snhwtlcwj_1/t1368899.htm. [hereinafter Position Paper].

165 Chinese government statements have indicated that in China's view both of the Tribunal's awards are "null and void" and has "no binding effect on China." See, China, 'Statement of the Ministry of Foreign Affairs on the Award on Jurisdiction and Admissibility of the South China Sea Arbitration by the Arbitral Tribunal Established at the Request of the Republic of the Philippines', 30 October 2015, on the Ministry of Foreign Affairs of China website available from www.fmprc.gov.cn/mfa_eng/zxxx_662805/t1310474.shtml; and, China, 'Statement of the Ministry of Foreign Affairs on the Award of 12 July 2016 of the Arbitral Tribunal Established at the Request of the Republic of the Philippines', 12 July 2016, on the Ministry of Foreign Affairs of China website available at, www.fmprc.gov.cn/nanhai/eng/snhwtlcwj_1/t1379492.htm.

166 See, South China Sea Arbitration, Award and Award on Jurisdiction and Admissibility (n 3).

167 LOSC, Article 288. See also, South China Sea Arbitration, Award (n 3), para. 167.

168 LOSC, Annex VII, Article 11.

presented by the Philippines and its experts alone. For example, the Tribunal appointed its own independent experts,[169] undertook research of its own of material in the public domain of China's practice in order to ascertain its position on issues to be adjudicated as well as inviting further comments from the parties to the case.[170] Further, the Tribunal was at pains to take into account China's official pronouncements whilst the case was ongoing, notably including China's Position Paper[171] which was issued shortly before a counter-Memorial would have been due to be delivered had China opted to participate in the case. The Tribunal also took into consideration *Amicus Curiae* submission of the Chinese (Taiwan) Society of International Law.[172]

3.1 *The Tribunal's Initial Considerations on the Status of Insular Features*

The Award of the Arbitral Tribunal in the case between the Philippines and China was delivered on 12 July 2016.[173] A substantial portion of the Award was devoted to the status of certain insular features in the South China Sea.[174]

---

169 Mr Grant Boyes of Geoscience Australia was appointed as the Tribunal's independent expert hydrographer. Additionally, expert reports were commissioned on navigational safety and coral reef issues. Ibid., paras 85 and 133.

170 See, South China Sea Arbitration, Award (n 3), paras 85–105 and 144. The practice of the South China Sea Tribunal with respect to appointing its own experts, while rare in cases before the ICJ, is not unique in the context of arbitration cases. For example, technical experts were appointed in both the Guyana-Suriname and Croatia-Slovenia cases. In contrast, where the ICJ did appoint a technical expert, in the Gulf of Maine case, it did so at the request of the parties to that case. See, In the Matter of an Arbitration between Guyana and Suriname, Award of the Arbitral Tribunal, ICGJ 370, PCA Case No 2004–04, 17 September 2007, Permanent Court of Arbitration [PCA], para. 108 and Appendix pp. A1–4, available at, https://pcacases.com/web/sendAttach/902; In the Matter of an Arbitration under the Arbitration Agreement between the Government of the Republic of Croatia and the Government of the Republic of Slovenia, signed on 4 November 2009, Final Award, PCA Case No. 2012–04, 29 June 2017, Permanent Court of Arbitration [PCA], paras 167–168; and, Delimitation of the Maritime Boundary in the Gulf of Maine Area (Canada/United States of America), Judgment of [1984] ICJ Reports, 246, ICGJ 120, 12 October 1984 International Court of Justice [ICJ].

171 Position Paper (n 164). While China did not formally participate in the South China Sea case, it arguably did so indirectly or informally as nonetheless the Tribunal took into account China's official statements and documents such as its Position Paper.

172 See, Chinese (Taiwan) Society of International Law, '*Amicus Curiae* Submission', 23 March 2016, available at csil.org.tw/home/wpcontent/uploads/2016/03/SCSTF-Amicus-Curiae-Brief-final.pdf; and, South China Sea Arbitration, Award (n 3), para. 449.

173 See, South China Sea Arbitration, Award (n 3).

174 Part VI of the Award encompasses 370 of 1,203 paragraphs and 142 of 479 pages (i.e., c.30 per cent of the Award as a whole).

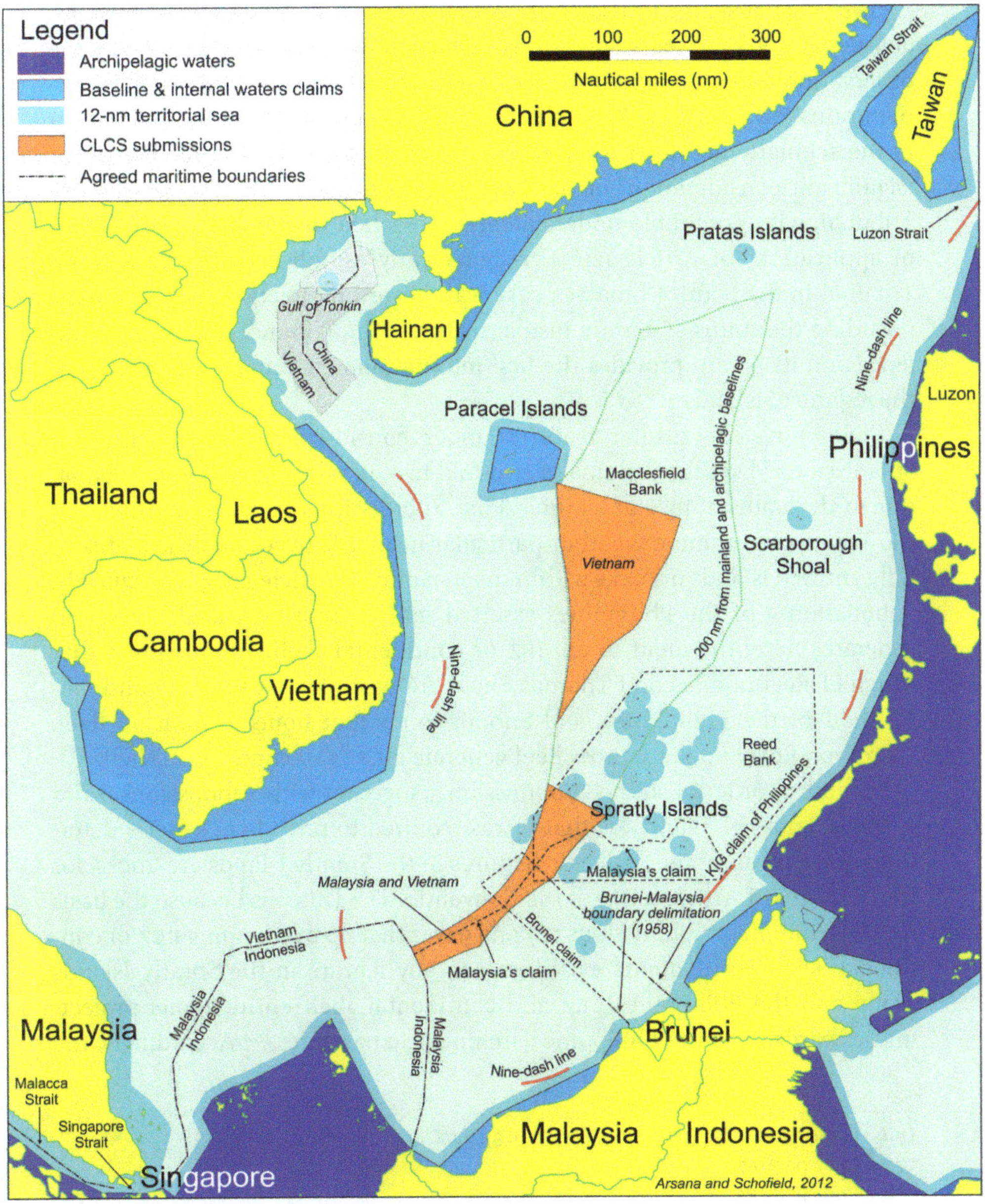

FIGURE 7 Maritime Claims in the South China Sea
SOURCE: ARSANA AND SCHOFIELD[175]

175 Adapted from map produced by IMA Arsana and CH Schofield in R Beckman and CH Schofield, 'Defining EEZ Claims from Islands: A Potential South China Sea Change' (2014) 29(2) *The International Journal of Marine and Coastal Law* 193–243, at 199.

As noted above, the provisions of Article 121 of LOSC have excited considerable debate over the years, something that the Tribunal acknowledged with the observation that commentators had reached "a wide range of different interpretations" on the issue.[176] In light of the diverse interpretations of Article 121 in the scholarly literature as well as in State practice and in the absence of "significant consideration" of the issue by courts and arbitral tribunals, The Tribunal, with admirable understatement, reached the view that "the scope of application" of Article 121(3) "is not clearly established."[177] The Arbitral Tribunal in the South China Sea case was, however, directly posed questions regarding the status of certain insular features. The Tribunal rose to this challenge and its Award provides the first international judicial interpretation of the regime of islands.

Concerning the insular features under consideration, the Philippines' Submissions[178] set the Tribunal a two-fold task in relation to the determination of the status of insular features. First, Submissions 5 and 7 requested that the Tribunal determine whether particular insular features had the status of fully entitled islands or rocks within the meaning of Article 121(3). Specifically, Submission 3 of the Philippines asserted that Scarborough Reef (or Shoal) generates no entitlement to an EEZ or continental shelf; Submission 5 that Mischief Reef and Second Thomas Shoal are part of the EEZ and continental shelf of the Philippines; and Submission 7 that none of Johnson Reef, Cuarteron Reef and Fiery Cross Reef generate an EEZ or continental shelf.[179]

Second, in order to address Submission 5, together with Submissions 8 and 9,[180] the Tribunal's view was that it was required to provide a "general determination that all of the high-tide features in the Spratly Islands are 'rocks' for the purposes of Article 121(3) of the Convention."[181] This was because the basis for the Philippines Submissions 5, 7 and 9 was that no overlapping EEZ or continental shelf entitlements exist between any feature in the Spratly Islands group and the Philippines EEZ and continental shelf entitlements projecting seawards from the Philippines archipelagic baselines.[182] Accordingly, the

176 South China Sea Arbitration, Award (n 3), para. 474.

177 Ibid., para, 474.

178 Ibid., para. 112

179 Ibid.

180 Ibid. Submission 8 requested that the Tribunal find that China had unlawfully interfered with the Philippines enjoyment of its EEZ and continental shelf rights in relation living and non-living resources whilst Submission 9 related to China having failed to prevent its national and vessels from exploiting living resources within the EEZ of the Philippines.

181 Ibid., para. 393.

182 Ibid., paras 395–396.

Tribunal assessed "all significant high-tide features in the Spratly Islands,"[183] including "a number of other features in the Spratly Islands that are unequivocally above water at high tide" but not specifically named in the Philippines Submissions.[184] These included Itu Aba, Thitu, West York Island, Spratly Island, North-East Cay and South-West Cay.[185] Although a number of other above high-tide features exist in the Spratly Islands which were not specifically ruled upon in its Award,[186] the Tribunal was of the view that if these six largest features were classified as rocks within the meaning of Article 121(3) then "the same conclusion would also hold true for all other high-tide features in the Spratly Islands."[187]

3.2 *The Tribunal's Interpretation of and Findings on Article 121*

The Tribunal observed that Article 121 comprises "a definition" of islands in paragraph one, "a general rule" at paragraph two and "an exception to that general rule" at paragraph three.[188] As noted above the Tribunal concluded that Article 121 contains a distinction between two categories of "naturally formed high-tide features", and referred to these as "fully entitled islands" and "rocks" under Article 121(2) and (3) respectively.

The Tribunal reviewed the positions of the parties on the regime of islands and their positions regarding islands in the South China Sea in particular. The Philippines position, in keeping with its Submissions, was that all of the South China Sea features that it had requested a ruling on the insular status of were rocks within the meaning of Article 121(3) of LOSC. As China did not participate in the case, the Tribunal sought to discern insights as to China's position on Article 121 by reference to its diplomatic statements on the subject. Here China's vigorous protests over the insular status of Japan's EEZ and continental shelf claims in relation to its tiny southernmost above high-water feature Okinotorishima arguably came back to haunt it. In this context the Tribunal noted China's "robust stance"[189] concerning the insular status of Okinotorishima, expressed through multiple *notes verbale* and other diplomatic statements. In particular the Tribunal took into account China's repeated assertions concerning the importance of the proper application of

183 Ibid., para. 396.
184 Ibid., para. 400.
185 Ibid., paras 401–406.
186 See, Lyons et al. (n 73), at 147 and 153.
187 South China Sea Arbitration, Award (n 3), para. 407.
188 Ibid., paras 387–390.
189 Ibid., para. 458.

Article 121(3) so as not to diminish or encroach upon the high seas and Area and thus the common heritage of all mankind.[190]

The Tribunal went on to apply Articles 31 and 32 of the Vienna Convention on the Law of Treaties in order to interpret Article 121 of the LOSC.[191] Article 31 of the VCLT provides that a treaty shall be "interpreted in good faith in accordance with the ordinary meaning to be given to the terms of the treaty in their context and in light of its object and purpose"[192] and taking into account, together with the context, "any subsequent agreement between the parties regarding the interpretation of the treaty or the application of its provisions"[193] and/or "any subsequent practice in the application of the treaty which establishes the agreement of the parties regarding its interpretation."[194] Moreover, Article 32 of the VCLT provides that "supplementary means of interpretation, including the preparatory work of the treaty and the circumstances of its conclusion"[195] may be used in order to determine the meaning of the treaty terms when the interpretation in accordance with Article 31 of the VCLT either leaves the meaning "ambiguous or obscure"[196] or "leads to a result which is manifestly absurd or unreasonable."[197] Accordingly, the Tribunal undertook a detailed analysis of Article 121 of the Convention encompassing a review and analysis of the text of the article with due attention given to the ordinary meaning of terms used within it, in their context, also in the light of the object and purpose of the Convention.

Firstly, regarding textual analysis, the Tribunal dealt with six *terms* – "rocks", "cannot", "sustain", "human habitation", "or", and "economic life of their own" – in succession, in order to interpret the ordinary meaning to be given to those terms which are used in Article 121(3).[198]

Secondly, the Tribunal analysed two aspects of the *context* of Article 121(3), in the light of the object and purpose of the Convention: (a) the context of islands, rocks and low-tide elevations (i.e., Articles 13 and 121); and (b) the link between Article 121(3) and the purpose of the exclusive economic zone.[199]

---

190 Ibid., paras and 451–458.

191 VCLT (n 15), Articles 31 and 32; South China Sea Arbitration, Award (n 3), para. 476.

192 Article 31(1) VCLT and South China Sea Arbitration, Award (n 3), para. 476.

193 Article 31(3)(a) VCLT.

194 Article 31(3)(b) VCLT. See also, South China Sea Arbitration, Award (n 3), para. 476.

195 Article 32 VCLT.

196 Ibid., Article 32(a).

197 Ibid., Article 32(b).

198 South China Sea Arbitration, Award (n 3), paras 478–506.

199 Ibid., paras 507–520.

Thirdly, the Tribunal, in accordance with Article 32 of the VCLT, also took into account *supplementary means* of interpretation, including the *travaux préparatoires*.[200] The Tribunal reached three conclusions in relation to the drafting history of Article 121. First, that Article 121(3) is a "provision of limitation" with the object and purpose of "preventing encroachment on the international seabed reserved for the common heritage of mankind and of avoiding the inequitable distribution of maritime spaces under national jurisdiction."[201] Second, that Article 121(3) was not discussed in isolation, but in concert with other aspects of the LOSC;[202] and third, that the drafters of the Convention accepted that the diversity of islands meant that "abstract, bright-line rules" applicable to all cases were difficult to establish, noting that "[p]roposals to introduce specific criteria were considered, but consistently rejected" – meaning that the language of compromise was preferred instead.[203] The Tribunal did, however, acknowledge that the *travaux préparatoires* for Article 121 are "an imperfect guide" given that "the key compromise" that yielded the text in question arose from "informal consultations in 1975, for which no records were kept."[204] Nevertheless, the Tribunal was of the view that some general conclusions would be drawn from the records available.[205]

As a result of this interpretative exercise the Tribunal reached nine general conclusions on the interpretation of Article 121(3) which in turn relate to the following key terms and concepts: rock, natural capacity, cannot, sustain, human habitation, economic life of their own, or, *and* present and past capacity, including the need to assess the capacity of an insular feature on a case-by-case basis.[206] Other conclusions also relate to the disjunctive nature of the text of Article 121(3), to the assessment with due regard to groups of small islands, and to evidence of physical conditions. The Tribunal then reverted

200 Ibid., paras 521–538.

201 Ibid., para. 535.

202 Notably the introduction and purpose of the EEZ "for the population of the coastal State" as well the introduction of the International Seabed Area, the common heritage of mankind, the interests of archipelagic States, the role of islands in the delimitation of maritime boundaries and concerns over the potential for artificial installations to generate maritime zones. See, ibid., para. 536.

203 Ibid., para. 537. With respect to island size specifically, the Tribunal noted that despite "repeated attempts" to categorise islands by size criteria, these were all rejected and that "although size may correlate to the availability of water, food, living space, and resources for an economic life – size cannot be dispositive of a feature's status as a fully entitled island or rock and is not, on its own, a relevant factor." See, ibid.

204 Ibid., para. 534.

205 Ibid.

206 Ibid., paras 539–553.

to interpretation in accordance with Article 31(3) of the VCLT, and analysed whether any *subsequent practice* in the application of the Convention by its parties might provide evidence of an agreement between them regarding interpretation of Article 121(3) which may differ from the interpretation of the Tribunal.

Turning to the main conclusions reached by the Tribunal in interpreting Article 121(3) as described above, the following sections summarize its key findings and relate these to the textual as well as contextual interpretation as contained in the Award.

3.2.1 Rock

First, the Tribunal found that the assessment of a particular feature was not to be based on geological or geomorphological criteria.[207] That is, that the term "rock" is not limited to features "composed of solid rock."[208] This finding appears to depart from the ordinary meaning of the word "rock".[209] However, the Tribunal noted that the dictionary definition of this word includes "aggregates", "organic matter" and "soft materials such as clays" rather than exclusively hard rock.[210] Here, the Tribunal drew support from the ICJ's finding in the Nicaragua-Colombia case that Article 121 could apply to a formation composed of coral boulders and that the term "rock" is defined by reference to its "naturally formed" character and whether it is "above water at high tide" and "not by reference to its geological composition" so that the fact that it is composed of coral is "irrelevant".[211]

The Tribunal observed that "rocks are a category of island", which is an important confirmation since this means that for a feature to be classified as a rock it needs to fulfil the requirements of Article 121(1) of the LOSC, that is, that the feature is "a naturally formed area of land, surrounded by water, which is above water at high tide" (see Section 2 above).[212] The Tribunal went on to clarify that Article 121(1) defines an island as a "naturally formed area of land"[213] and does so "without any geological or geomorphological qualification."[214]

The Tribunal was robust in its view that, "imposing a geological criteria on Article 121(3) would lead to an absurd result", whereby above high-tide features

207 Ibid., para. 540.
208 Ibid.
209 See, for example, Prescott and Schofield (n 17), 61–63.
210 Oxford English Dictionary, quoted in ibid., para. 480.
211 Nicaragua-Colombia case (n 41), para. 37.
212 LOSC, Article 121(1). South China Sea Arbitration, Award (n 3), para. 481.
213 LOSC, Article 121(1).
214 South China Sea Arbitration, Award (n 3), para. 480.

composed of non-rocky, softer materials would always generate extended maritime entitlements, that is EEZ and continental shelf rights, regardless of whether they were capable of sustaining human habitation or an economic life of their own" and that this "cannot have been the intent of the Article."[215] This purposive interpretation of the Tribunal accords with the Tribunal's view that fundamental intention of Article 121(3) was as a provision of limitation.[216] That is, the imposition of a geological criterion would defeat this objective and render the provision to be nonsensical if features composed of solid rock were to be excluded from fully entitled island status yet features of equivalent or lesser size but composed of other materials such as sand, coral or mud were exempt from the limiting effect of Article 121(3).

The Tribunal therefore stated in explicit terms that its interpretation on this point meant that "'rocks' for the purposes of Article 121(3) will not necessarily be composed of rock"[217] and that "the use of the word 'rock' does not limit the provision to features composed of solid rock" as the "geological and geomorphological characteristics of a high tide feature are not relevant to its classification pursuant to Article 121(3)" of the LOSC.[218] The Tribunal also stated that toponyms, that is whether a feature was called a rock or an island, had "no bearing" on whether a particular feature qualifies as a rock within the meaning of Article 121(3) of the LOSC.[219]

The Tribunal also noted ICJ's ruling in the Nicaragua-Colombia case that "international law does not prescribe any minimum size which a feature must possess in order to be considered an island"[220] in support of its own finding that "size cannot be dispositive of a feature's status as a fully entitled island or rock and is not, on its own, a relevant factor", even if island size "may correlate to the availability of water, food, living space, and resources for an economic life."[221]

215 Ibid., para. 481.
216 See, Gullett (n 126), at 13.
217 South China Sea Arbitration, Award (n 3), para. 482.
218 Ibid., para. 540.
219 Ibid., para. 482. The Tribunal also noted that if a feature was called a reef or a shoal it "may have protrusions that remain exposed at high tide" meaning that the feature would be legally a rock – a comment seemingly made with Scarborough Reef in mind which is a largely submerged atoll with 5–7 rocks exposed at high-tide located on it. See, ibid., paras 554–556.
220 Nicaragua-Colombia case (n 41), para. 37; and, South China Sea Arbitration, Award (n 3), para. 538.
221 South China Sea Arbitration, Award (n 3), para. 538.

3.2.2 Natural Capacity

Next, the Tribunal emphasised that "[t]he status of a feature must be assessed on the basis of its natural condition."[222] Thus, assessment of a particular insular feature should be determined on the basis of the feature's "natural capacity" to sustain human habitation or an economic life of its own, "without external additions or modifications intended to increase its capacity" to do so.[223] In particular, the Tribunal pointed to the phrasing of both Articles 13 and 121, dealing with low-tide elevations and rocks respectively, that these features comprise a "natural formed area of land" as an important qualification.

In interpreting Article 121(3) the Tribunal set this provision in the context of the system and hierarchy of classifying insular features (islands, rocks, and low-tide elevations) and was explicit in its view that:

> Just as a low-tide elevation or area of seabed cannot be legally transformed into an island through human efforts, the Tribunal considers that a rock cannot be transformed into a fully entitled island through land reclamation.[224]

The Tribunal once again focussed on the object and purpose of Article 121(3) as being a "provision of limitation" – an objective which would be frustrated if States "were allowed to convert any rock incapable of sustaining human habitation or an economic life into a fully entitled island simply by the introduction of technology and extraneous materials."[225] Here the Tribunal agreed with the argument of the Philippines that:

> [a] contrary rule would create perverse incentives for States to undertake such actions to extend their maritime zones to the detriment of other coastal States and/or the common heritage of mankind.[226]

The Tribunal acknowledged that for many of the insular features in the South China Sea subject to the case, substantial modifications and construction had taken place on them such that "it is now difficult to observe directly the original status of the feature in its natural state."[227] In such circumstances the Tribunal advocated the determination of the status of a feature based on

222 Ibid., para. 508.
223 Ibid., para. 541.
224 Ibid., para. 508.
225 Ibid., para. 509.
226 Quoted in ibid.
227 South China Sea Arbitration, Award (n 3), para. 511.

best available evidence of its natural condition "prior to the onset of significant human modification".[228]

3.2.3 Cannot

The Tribunal's third and fourth findings related to whether a feature can or cannot "sustain human habitation or an economic life of their own" in keeping with Article 121(3) of the LOSC.[229] The word "cannot" appearing immediately before "sustain human habitation or economic life" in Article 121(3) was viewed by the Tribunal as indicating "a concept of capacity".[230] This was framed through the question: "Does the feature in its natural form have the capability of sustaining human habitation or an economic life?";[231] and the legal consequence under Article 121(3): "If not, it is a rock."[232] The Tribunal made it clear that whether a particular feature is presently inhabited or has an economic life of its own is immaterial as "the fact that a feature is currently not inhabited does not prove that it is uninhabitable" and similarly, "the fact that it has no economic life does not prove that it cannot sustain an economic life".[233] Instead, the issue is "whether, objectively, the feature is apt, able to, or lends itself to human habitation or economic life."[234] Historical evidence of human habitation and economic life were viewed by the Tribunal as potentially relevant to establishing a features capacity in this regard.[235]

3.2.4 Sustain

With respect to the meaning of the word "sustain", the Tribunal once again referred to the ordinary meaning of the word, as a starting point, that is, to "support, maintain or uphold" and "for an extended period or without interruption."[236] Further, with respect to a place, the ordinary meaning taken into account by the Tribunal was that "sustain" means to provide "food, drink, and other necessities."[237] The Tribunal took a three-fold understanding of "sustain" from the ordinary meaning – a need to provide the "support and provision of essentials"; a temporal aspect whereby such support must be sustained

228 Ibid.
229 Ibid., para. 542–543.
230 Ibid., para. 483.
231 Ibid.
232 Ibid.
233 Ibid.
234 Ibid.
235 Ibid., para. 484.
236 Oxford English Dictionary, quoted in ibid., para. 485.
237 Ibid., para. 486.

over time and not "one-off or short-lived"; and thirdly a qualitative concept of "entailing at least a minimal 'proper standard'.[238] This led the Tribunal to conclude that:

> Thus, in connection with sustaining human habitation, to "sustain" means to provide that which is necessary to keep humans alive and healthy over a continuous period of time, according to a proper standard. In connection with an economic life, to "sustain" means to provide that which is necessary not just to commence, but also to continue, an activity over a period of time in a way that remains viable on an ongoing basis.

This interpretation of "sustain" logically relies on the ordinary meaning of the term and is linked to human habitation (see below). It does, however, introduce fresh terms capable of varied interpretation. In particular, while the spirit of the requirement that a population be sustained "to a proper standard" is clear, an objective test is lacking and is open to multiple interpretations. The counterpoint on here is that this interpretation provides the flexibility necessary for general application and avoids arbitrary tests.

3.2.5 Human Habitation

Concerning the phrase "human habitation", the Tribunal was of the view that "[t]he mere presence of a small number of persons on a feature does not constitute permanent or habitual residence there and does not equate to habitation."[239] It was also found that the "critical factor" was that this be "non-transient [in] character" such that the inhabitants "can fairly be said to constitute the natural population of the feature."[240]

The Tribunal, based once again on a dictionary definition, took the objective meaning of human habitation to be centred around terms including "dwelling", "inhabiting", "occupancy", "to reside in" and "permanently or habitually".[241] In an important interpretive clarification, the Tribunal concluded that the term "habitation" includes both temporal and qualitative elements reflected in "the notions of settlement and residence that are inherent in that term."[242] Thus, the "mere presence of a small number of persons on a feature does not constitute permanent or habitual residence there and does not equate to habitation."[243]

238 Ibid., para. 487.
239 Ibid., para. 489.
240 Ibid., para. 542
241 Ibid., para. 488, relying on the Oxford English Dictionary.
242 Ibid., para. 489.
243 Ibid.

Instead, the "non-transient presence of persons who have chosen to stay and reside on the feature in a settled manner" is required.[244] Consequently, for a feature to be deemed capable of human habitation it needs to provide not just "all of the elements necessary to keep people alive on the feature",[245] but conditions "sufficiently conducive" for human life and livelihood upon it.[246]

This qualitative element in assessing human habitation would seem to be open to variable interpretation, especially given the diversity of islands and socio-economic as well as cultural factors worldwide. Indeed, the Tribunal acknowledged the great variation in the forms of human habitation globally, indicating that for an international instrument such as the LOSC, "no particular culture or mode of habitation should be assumed" for the assessment of a feature in relation to insular status.[247] Nonetheless, the Tribunal was of the view that particular aspects of habitation by humans "remain constant" wherever it occurs such that:

> At a minimum, sustained human habitation would require that a feature be able to support, maintain, and provide food, drink, and shelter to some humans to enable them to reside there permanently or habitually over an extended period of time.[248]

Following on from this finding, the Tribunal expressed the view that the term "habitation" also "generally implies" the habitation of a particular feature "by a group or community of persons."[249] It was, however, immediately observed that Article 121(3) does not directly indicate the threshold to distinguish "settled human habitation" from the "mere presence of humans."[250] Similarly, the text of the provision fails to specify the "physical characteristics of a feature" required to "sustain the more settled mode of human habitation", as opposed to "merely ensuring human survival."[251]

Thus, while the Tribunal reached the conclusion that a "qualitative aspect is apparent" in Article 121(3), it acknowledged that the provision "is not specific with respect to the threshold separating human habitation from mere extended presence of humans" and that the text "offers little guidance as to

244 Ibid.
245 Ibid.
246 Ibid.
247 Ibid., para. 490.
248 Ibid.
249 Ibid., para. 491.
250 Ibid., para. 492.
251 Ibid.

where this line should be drawn."[252] The Tribunal did, however, link the capacity of an insular feature to generate EEZ rights to the presence of a population to benefit from the resources within that zone, with the "critical factor" viewed as:

> ... the non-transient character of the inhabitation, such that the inhabitants can fairly be said to constitute the natural population of the feature, for whose benefit the resources of the exclusive economic zone were seen to merit protection.[253]

The Tribunal went on to explain that "human habitation" was to be understood as involving "the inhabitation of the feature by a stable community of people for whom the feature constitutes a home and on which they can remain."[254] The requirement for a "stable community" of people to be present on an island for it to fulfil the human habitation criteria and thus be able to generate EEZ and continental shelf entitlements echoes both Van Dyke and Bennett suggestions dating from 1993[255] and, perhaps more tellingly, the above-mentioned and more recent Declaration of Judge Vukas in the Volga case.[256] However, the phrase "a stable community of people" was not qualified by any objective test and so is open to varied interpretation (see further in Section VI, below).

This finding, as well as that concerning economic life of a feature was founded on the Tribunal's considerations on the context in which Article 121(3) was drafted and the fundamental object and purpose of the provision and was clearly conscious here of the needs of small island States (see further below).

3.2.6 Economic Life of Their Own

The Tribunal viewed the term "economic life of their own" to be linked to the presence of a population as the economic life of a feature "will ordinarily be the life and livelihoods of the human population inhabiting and making its home" on an insular feature or group of features.[257]

The Tribunal took the ordinary meaning of the term "economic" to be "relating to the development and regulation of the material resources of a

252 Ibid., 505.
253 Ibid., para. 542.
254 Ibid.
255 JM Van Dyke and D Bennett, 'Islands and the Delimitation of Ocean Space in the South China Sea' (1993) 10 *Ocean Yearbook* 54–89, at 79.
256 The Volga case (n 124), Declaration of Vice-President Vukas.
257 Ibid., para. 543.

community."[258] With regard to the "life" component of "economic life", the Tribunal reasoned that this term suggests that "the mere presence of resources will be insufficient" and that "some level of local human activity" is also needed in relation to the exploitation, development and distribution of such resources in order to constitute an economic life.[259] Moreover, the Tribunal viewed the "economic life" requirement as having a temporal dimension such that "ongoing economic activity" must exist and further that there should be "a basic level of viability" for that activity, despite the absence of any reference to value in the text of Article 121(3).[260]

The phrase "of their own", was viewed by the Tribunal as being "essential" to its interpretation as:

> it makes clear that a feature itself (or group of related features) must have the ability to support an independent economic life, without relying predominantly on the infusion of outside resources or serving purely as an object for extractive activities, without the involvement of a local population.[261]

In considering economic activity related to sea areas adjacent to an insular feature, the Tribunal distinguished between activities in the possible EEZ and continental shelf of a feature and those occurring in its territorial sea. With respect to economic activities derived from a possible EEZ the Tribunal rule that these "must necessarily be excluded" as it would be "circular and absurd" if activities within a potential EEZ or continental shelf were themselves "sufficient to endow a feature with those very zones."[262]

In contrast, no circularity would occur in relation to economic activities within the territorial sea as, so long as the conditions of Article 121(1) are met, any island generates a territorial sea. Nonetheless, in the Tribunal's view the terminology "of its own" entails a requirement for "a link between the economic life and the feature itself, rather than merely its adjacent waters."[263] Consequently,

258 Ibid., para. 499, relying on the *Shorter Oxford English Dictionary*.
259 Ibid.
260 Ibid.
261 Ibid., para. 500.
262 Ibid., para. 502.
263 Ibid., para. 503.

> Distant fisherman exploiting the territorial sea surrounding a small rock and making no use of the feature itself, however, would not suffice to give the feature an economic life of its own. Nor would an enterprise devoted to extracting the mineral resources of the seabed adjacent to such a feature and making no use of the feature itself.[264]

In keeping with the reasoning that economic life will in most instances "go hand in hand" with human habitation, the Tribunal determined that the phrase did not refer to the economic value of the feature itself.[265] Moreover, the economic activity involved in qualifying as "economic life of their own" should be "oriented around the feature itself and not focused solely on the waters or seabed of the surrounding territorial sea" and not entirely dependent on outside resources; as the Tribunal stated:

> Economic activity that is entirely dependent on external resources or devoted to using a feature as an object for extractive activities without the involvement of a local population would also fall inherently short with respect to this necessary link to the feature itself.[266]

Thus, economic activity could form part of the economic life of a feature but only if "it is somehow linked to the feature itself, whether through a local population or otherwise".[267] A problematic issue in this context is that most, if not all, islands and the communities living on them are reliant to some extent on the provision of external supplies and support. Here the Tribunal observed that while "[t]rade and links with the outside world do not disqualify a feature to the extent that they go to improving the quality of life of its inhabitants", this is distinct from the scenario where "outside support is so significant that it constitutes a necessary condition for the inhabitation of a feature", in which case "it is no longer the feature itself that sustains human habitation."[268] Objective guidance on the threshold where external support becomes so significant as to be an essential or necessary condition for human habitation is, however, lacking. The Tribunal considered that evidence of the historical use and habitation of a feature, thus it being "capable of sustaining human habitation" to be "the most reliable" historical evidence

264 Ibid.
265 Ibid., para. 543
266 Ibid.
267 Ibid., para. 503.
268 Ibid., para. 550.

in establishing the status of a feature in its natural state, prior to significant technological intervention.[269]

The Tribunal's interpretation of the phrase "of its own" as meaning that economic activities needed to be related to either the feature itself or its territorial sea and, critically, linking this activity to the benefit of the local community living on a feature is an important development. This aspect of the Tribunal's ruling is founded on the Tribunal's understanding of the purpose of Article 121(3) as a "provision of limitation"[270] and assists in clarifying when this limitation, the status of a rock rather than a fully entitled island, should be applied. What is arguably less clear is whether the status of a feature may change as technology changes and thus different forms of economic activity become possible – something that is likely to become increasingly challenging in the future.

3.2.7 Or

Building on the above finding, the Tribunal also concluded that the text of Article 121(3) is disjunctive, meaning that either capacity to sustain human habitation or economic life of its own is required in order for a feature to escape being classified as a "rock".[271] The Philippines had argued that a feature must be able to support both human habitation and an economic life of its own.[272] The Tribunal disagreed, finding that the although the Philippines was correct to point to the provision creating "cumulative requirement", the logical structure and emphasis of the provision related to a feature being denied an exclusive economic zone and continental shelf, meaning that "if a feature is capable of sustaining either human habitation or an economic life of its own, it will qualify as a fully entitled island."[273]

While the Tribunal was conscious that "formal logic accords imperfectly with linguistic usage at the best of times, even among legal drafters" and was therefore "hesitant to accord decisive weight to logical construction alone",[274] it found that the structure of the remainder of Article 121(3) "foreclosed" the Philippines' interpretation as it would be "manifestly absurd and contrary to the clear intent of the Article" if a rock were to generate entitlement to one or other of an EEZ or continental shelf but not both.[275] Thus, the Tribunal concluded that:

269 Ibid., para. 549.
270 Ibid., para. 535.
271 This finding represented the Tribunal's fifth conclusion. Ibid., para. 544.
272 Ibid., para. 493.
273 Ibid., para. 494.
274 Ibid., para. 495.
275 Ibid.

> … properly interpreted, a rock would be disentitled from an exclusive economic zone and continental shelf only if it were to lack *both* the capacity to sustain human habitation *and* the capacity to sustain an economic life of its own. Or, expressed more straightforwardly and in positive terms, an island that is able to sustain *either* human habitation *or* an economic life of its own is entitled to *both* an exclusive economic zone *and* a continental shelf (in accordance with the provisions of the Convention applicable to other land territory).[276]

The Tribunal observed that the wording of Article 121(3):

> … remains open to the possibility that a feature may be able to sustain human habitation but offer no resources to support an economic life, or that a feature may sustain an economic life while lacking the conditions necessary to sustain [human] habitation directly on the feature itself.[277]

That said, the Tribunal indicated that because "economic activity is carried out by humans" who "will rarely inhabit areas where no economic activity or livelihood is possible" the two concepts are effectively "linked in practical terms" and thus in effect conflated.[278]

3.2.8 Present and Past Capacity

The Tribunal concluded that the assessment of insular features concerns their capacity to sustain human habitation or economic life rather than whether a feature is presently or has historically done so and that this did not depend on any prior decision on sovereignty over the feature.[279] In this context, as noted earlier, the Tribunal considered that evidence relating to the historical use to which it has been put was "the most reliable" for the assessment of a feature's capacity to sustain human habitation or an economic life of its own.[280]

3.2.9 Assessment on a Case-by-Case Basis

The Tribunal emphasised that assessment of an insular feature's capacity for human habitation or an economic life of its own "must be assessed on a case-by-case basis".[281] In its review of the drafting history of Article 121, the

276 Ibid., para. 496 (emphases in original).
277 Ibid., para. 497.
278 Ibid.
279 Ibid., para. 545.
280 Ibid., para. 549.
281 Ibid., para. 546.

Tribunal noted the diversity of islands alluded to at the outset of this study and commented on the similarly multitudinous proposals made for objective tests based on island size, proximity, population and physical characteristics to distinguish between fully entitled and disadvantaged features made during the negotiations at UNCLOS III – all of which were in vain.[282] Here the Tribunal observed that "the negotiating history clearly demonstrates the difficulty in setting, in the abstract, bright-line rules for all cases."[283]

Nonetheless, the Tribunal was of the view that "the principal factors" contributing to the natural capacity of a feature to support human habitation or an economic life of its own can be identified and went on to list "the presence of water, food, and shelter in sufficient quantities to enable a group of persons to live on the feature for an indeterminate period of time."[284] It was noted that other considerations could be taken into account in the assessment, including the prevailing climate, the proximity of the feature to other settled areas and the rather general consideration of "the potential for livelihoods on or around the feature."[285] Variability in these factors between features was acknowledged with the Tribunal therefore reaching the view that it "does not consider that an abstract test of the objective requirements to sustain human habitation or economic life can or should be formulated."[286] This finding offers necessary interpretational flexibility in order to accommodate the assessment of the enormous diversity of insular features throughout the global ocean.

3.2.10 Groups of Islands Sustaining Human Habitation and Economic Life

As noted above, the Tribunal was sensitive to the needs of small island States. Accordingly, the Tribunal concluded that the capacity of a feature to sustain human habitation or economic life should be assessed "with due regard to the potential for a group of small island features to collectively sustain human habitation and economic life."[287] In particular, the Tribunal stated that it was "conscious that remote island populations often make use of a number of islands, sometimes spread over significant distances, for sustenance and livelihoods."[288] In consequence, the Tribunal found that:

282 Ibid., paras 537 and 546.
283 Ibid., para. 537.
284 Ibid., para. 546.
285 Ibid., para. 546.
286 Ibid.
287 Ibid., para. 547.
288 Ibid.

> … provided that such islands collectively form part of a network that sustains human habitation in keeping with the traditional lifestyle of the peoples in question, the Tribunal would not equate the role of multiple islands in this manner with external supply. Nor would the local use of nearby resources as part of the livelihood of the community equate to the arrival of distant economic interests aimed at extracting natural resources.[289]

This recognition of the vulnerabilities and requirements of small island States is certainly welcome (see Section 6.4). It does, however, pose interpretational challenges for the future. As noted above, the Tribunal's Award provides no objective test or limit on how many islands might make up a network used collectively to sustain human habitation or economic life nor how far dispersed they may be though the Tribunal's mention of "significant distances" potentially implies hundreds of miles or more.[290] Similarly, the Award is silent on how the phrase "traditional lifestyle" is to be defined. Disputes over the meaning of the term "traditional fishing" suggest that this may be the source of future contention.[291]

3.2.11 Borderline Cases

The Tribunal further observed that evidence of the physical characteristics of a particular insular feature could take it "only so far." Thus, while evidence of physical conditions would "ordinarily suffice" to make a determination whether a feature should be classified as a fully entitled feature or a mere rock within the meaning of Article 121(3) of the LOSC, this may not be sufficient for "features that fall close to the line."[292] Accordingly, physical conditions alone may be insufficient to determine "where the capacity merely to keep people alive ends and the capacity to sustain settled habitation by a human community begins."[293] This is especially the case, the Tribunal noted, as the "relevant threshold may differ from one feature to another."[294] Here, the Tribunal appears to offer further scope for interpretational leeway and underscored the need for features to be assessed on a case-by-case basis.

---

289 Ibid.

290 For example, the people of seafaring communities such as those of the Pacific range over thousands of miles.

291 See, for example, BM Tsamenyi, 'Managing Indonesian Traditional Fishing in Australian Waters: An Australian Perspective' 86 (1996) *Maritime Studies* 18–26.

292 South China Sea Arbitration, Award (n 3), para. 548.

293 Ibid.

294 Ibid.

3.2.12 Context of Article 121(3) and the Object and Purpose of the LOSC

Of particular note, the Tribunal linked the capacity of an insular feature to generate EEZ rights to the purpose of the EEZ.[295] The Tribunal reasoned that the meaning of the text of Article 121(3) is "shaped by its context" and "the inherent connection between this provision and the concept of the exclusive economic zone" and further that "[t]he genesis of that Article is inextricably linked with the expansion of coastal State jurisdiction" through the EEZ.[296] Here, the Tribunal referred to the history of the Convention to reach the conclusion that the Article 121(3) was included in the Convention as a "counterpoint" to the introduction of the EEZ serving to prevent the expansion in maritime rights provided by the EEZ "from going too far" by disabling tiny features from:

> ... unfairly and inequitably generating enormous entitlements to maritime space that would serve not to benefit the local population, but to award windfall to the (potentially distant) State to have maintained a claim to such a feature.[297]

Against this context, the Tribunal considered that "the meaning attributed to the terms of Article 121(3) should serve to reinforce ... the purposes that the exclusive economic zone *and* Article 121(3) were respectively intended to serve".[298] The Tribunal was of the view that this is:

> ... best accomplished by recognising the connection between the criteria of "human habitation" and the population of the coastal State for the benefit of whom the resources of the exclusive economic zone were to be preserved.[299]

The Tribunal stated that this connection was not "narrowly intended" but rather that, "without human habitation (or an economic life), the link between a maritime feature and the people of the coastal State becomes increasingly slight."[300] The Tribunal supported this view by reference to a comment from the representative of Peru made during the Seabed Committee to illustrate that it was recognised that 200 M zone limits should not:

295 Ibid., para. 512.
296 Ibid.
297 Ibid., para. 516.
298 South China Sea Arbitration, Award (n 3), para. 512.
299 Ibid., para. 517.
300 Ibid.

> be applied to more or less uninhabited islands, since its main justification lay not in the existence of a territory but in the presence of the population which inhabited it, whose needs should be satisfied through the use of the resources available in its environs.[301]

Moreover, the Tribunal quoted a comment on the part of Ambassador Tommy Koh, who later served as President of UNCLOS III, that:

> The rationale for the proposal that coastal States should have the right to establish an economic zone was essentially based upon the interests of the people and the desire to marshal the resources of ocean space for their development ... However, it would be unjust, and the common heritage of mankind would be further diminished, if every island, irrespective of its characteristics, was automatically entitled to claim a uniform economic zone. Such an approach would give inequitable benefits to coastal States with small or uninhabited islands scattered over a wide expanse of the ocean. The economic zone of a barren rock would be larger than the land territory of many States and larger than the economic zones of many coastal States.[302]

These considerations led the Tribunal to conclude that:

> ... the human habitation with which the drafters of Article 121(3) were concerned was the habitation by a portion of the population for whose benefit the exclusive economic zone was being introduced.[303]

In combination with notions the Tribunal's findings concerning the meaning of "settlement and residence" as well as its view regarding "the qualitative aspect inherent in the term habitation", human habitation of a feature should therefore be understood to be by "a settled group or community for whom the feature is a home."[304]

The Tribunal also took into account the *travaux préparatoires* as they relate to Article 121(3). The Tribunal noted that, prior to the 1970s, the issue of very small high-tide features generating expansive continental shelf claims had yet to become urgent but this situation changed "from 1971" and the definition of

301 Ibid., para. 518.
302 Ibid., para. 519.
303 Ibid., para. 520.
304 Ibid.

islands and their maritime entitlements took on a new relevance in the context of the emerging regime of expanded maritime entitlements. In particular, the Tribunal noted concerns expressed by Ambassador Arvid Pardo of Malta regarding "the prospect of granting such entitlements to all islands without distinction"[305] as follows:

> If a 200 mile limit of jurisdiction could be founded on the possession of uninhabited, remote or very small islands, the effectiveness of international administration of ocean space beyond a national jurisdiction would be gravely impaired.[306]

The Tribunal noted the debates over Article 121(3) at UNCLOS III and the difficulty of reaching a "workable formula",[307] leading to the compromise text that became Article 121(3). While efforts were made to amend this text and excise the third paragraph from Article 121 entirely, the Tribunal noted that these were rejected and included comments from the Danish representative at the 11th session of UNCLOS III (April 1982), who emphasised that without Article 121(3):

> tiny and barren islands, looked upon in the past as mere obstacles to navigation, would miraculously become the golden keys to vast maritime zones. That would indeed be an unwarranted and unacceptable consequence of the new law of the sea.[308]

Similarly, the Tribunal referred to a statement by the representative of Colombia at the same session of UNCLOS III, who stated that Article 121 reflected: "a unique and delicate balance and would help to preserve the common heritage in the oceans."[309]

Drawing on the *travaux préparatoires*, the Tribunal determined that Article 121(3) is a "provision of limitation" with "the object and purpose of preventing encroachment on the international seabed reserved for the common heritage of mankind and of avoiding the inequitable distribution of maritime spaces under national jurisdiction."[310] This was an interpretation that the Tribunal considered to be consistent with the views of the Philippines in its

305 Ibid., para. 526.
306 Ibid.
307 Ibid., para. 530.
308 Ibid., para. 533
309 Ibid.
310 Ibid., para. 535.

pleadings as well as China's, based on its past practice and aforementioned diplomatic correspondence particularly concerning the status of Japan's Okinotorishima (see above).[311]

The Tribunal went on to determine that only features with a capacity to sustain either "a stable community of people",[312] for whom the feature constitutes a home[313] should qualify as islands capable of generating EEZ and continental shelf rights. As noted above, no indication was provided as to how many people might constitute such a stable community of people and over what time span they would need to make an island their home, however.

The Tribunal further clarified that "a purely official or military population, serviced from the outside, does not constitute evidence that a feature is capable of sustaining human habitation."[314] This was a vital distinction in the context of the South China Sea, where all of the claimant States, save for Brunei, maintains garrisons on at least one of the disputed Spratly Islands. This ruling was made in keeping with the purpose of Article 121(3) "to place limits on excessive and unfair claims by States", something that would be "undermined if a population were installed on a feature that, as such, would not be capable of sustaining human habitation, precisely to stake a claim to the territory and the maritime zones generated by it."[315] Consequently, the Tribunal viewed evidence of human habitation prior to the creation of EEZs to be more compelling than contemporary evidence which may be potentially "clouded by an apparent attempt to assert a maritime claim."[316]

3.3 *Application to the Spratly Islands and Scarborough Reef*

Although in its submissions the Philippines had initially requested that the Tribunal confine its considerations on the status of insular features in the South China Sea to specific, named, features,[317] the Tribunal instead decided to take into consideration the Spratly Islands group as a whole. The Tribunal did so because the Philippines had also requested that the Tribunal rule on whether China had infringed its sovereign rights in its EEZ and continental shelf. As

311 Ibid.
312 Ibid., para 542.
313 Ibid.
314 Ibid., para. 550.
315 Ibid.
316 Ibid.
317 Namely, Scarborough Shoal, Mischief Reef, Second Thomas Shoal, Subi Reef, Gaven Reef, McKennan Reef (including Hughes Reef), Johnson Reef, Cuarteron Reef, Fiery Cross Reef. See, ibid., para. 112.

the Tribunal was prohibited as a consequence of China's 2006 Declaration[318] from addressing maritime delimitation issues, the Tribunal could only address the Philippines submission concerning its EEZ and continental shelf rights if it was confident that no overlapping entitlements between China and the Philippines existed in the areas under consideration. Moreover, due to the location of the Spratly Islands coupled with the geographical dimensions of the South China Sea, this conclusion could only be reached if none of the disputed, above high-tide of the Spratly Islands capable of generating 200 M EEZ and continental shelf rights.

Accordingly, the Tribunal applied its above-detailed reasoning with respect to distinguishing between fully entitled islands and rocks within the meaning of Article 121(3) and undertook an extensive review of evidence concerning the capacity of above high-tide features among the Spratly Islands to sustain human habitation or an economic life of their own. Here it is important to note that the Tribunal did not rely solely on the evidence presented by the Philippines but commissioned its own research from publically available sources including the United Kingdom Hydrographic Office and France's *Bibliothèque Nationale de France* and *Archives Nationales d'Outre-Mer*.[319] The Tribunal went on to note that all of the more significant above high-tide features in the Spratly Islands are occupied by one of the South China Sea coastal States, that construction had taken place on these features and personnel had been installed there. However, this presence was determined to be "predominantly military or governmental in nature and involves significant outside supply".[320]

The Tribunal added that "many of the high-tide features have been significantly modified from their natural condition" and was wary of "deliberate attempts to colour the description" of features so as to "enhance or reduce the likelihood of the feature being considered to generate an exclusive economic zone, depending on the interests of the State in question."[321] This resulted in the Tribunal relying on historical evidence of conditions on features "prior to the advent of the exclusive economic zone as a concept or the beginning of significant human modification" as a "more reliable guide to the capacity of the features to sustain human habitation or economic life."[322]

The Tribunal then proceeded to review a number of factors relating to the Spratly Islands, namely, the availability of potable fresh water,[323] vegetation and

318 See UNTC (n 163).
319 South China Sea Arbitration, Award (n 3), para. 577.
320 Ibid., para. 578.
321 Ibid.
322 Ibid.
323 Ibid., paras 580–584.

biology,[324] soil and agricultural potential,[325] the presence of fishermen,[326] and commercial operations.[327] This assessment included the larger features in the Spratly Islands group such as Itu Aba (Taiping Island) which is reportedly only 1.4 km in length and 370 m across.[328]

On the basis of this review the Tribunal ruled that the principal above high-tide features of the Spratly Islands "are capable of enabling the survival of small groups of people" based on historic evidence relating to the availability of potable water, albeit of "variable quality", the presence of vegetation "capable of providing shelter", the potential for "at least limited agriculture to supplement the food resources of the surrounding waters" and evidence of the presence. Of "small numbers of fishermen, mainly from Hainan" on Itu Aba and the other larger features.[329] Although the Tribunal was of the view that these features "are not barren rocks or sand cays, devoid of fresh water" that can be readily dismissed as uninhabitable on the basis of their physical characteristics alone, nonetheless they "are not obviously habitable, and their capacity even to enable human survival appears to be distinctly limited."[330] Here it can be noted that, prior to China's large-scale island-building campaign, the combined estimated land area of the largest 12 above high-tide features of Spratly Islands was less than 2 km^2.[331] As noted above, although size is not a determinative factor for fully entitled island status in accordance with Article 121(2), nonetheless island size retains a residual role as some space is needed to provide a basis for human habitation and an economic life, and their small size is suggestive that they are marginal in this respect.

As such the Spratly Islands were viewed as being features that "fall close to the line in terms of their capacity to sustain human habitation,"[332] and the

324 Ibid., paras 585–593.

325 Ibid., paras 594–596.

326 Ibid., paras 597–601.

327 Ibid., paras 602–614.

328 See, D Hancox and JRV Prescott, *A Geographical Description of the Spratly Islands and An Account of Hydrographic Surveys Amongst Those Islands*, Maritime Briefing, 1(6) (International Boundaries Research Unit: Durham, 1995), at 8. See also, D Hancox and JRV Prescott, *Secret Hydrographic Surveys in the Spratly Islands*, (The Maritime Institute of Malaysia: Kuala Lumpur, 1997); and CH Schofield, 'Dangerous Ground – A Geopolitical Overview of the South China Sea' in S Bateman and R Emmers (eds), *Security and International Politics in the South China Sea: Towards a Co-operative Management Regime* (Routledge: London, 2009) 7–25, at 9.

329 South China Sea Arbitration, Award (n 3), para. 615.

330 Ibid., para. 616.

331 Beckman and Schofield (n 175), at 210.

332 South China Sea Arbitration, Award (n 3), para. 616.

Tribunal considered that the physical characteristics of these features do not definitively indicate their capacity even to enable human survival.[333] Further, with respect to historical evidence of human habitation and economic life on the Spratly Islands, the Tribunal was unconvinced[334] and ruled out the presence of military and other government personnel deployed to the Spratly Islands as being sufficient "to constitute 'human habitation' for the purposes of Article 121(3)."[335] Consequently, the Tribunal concluded that it saw "no indication that anything fairly resembling a stable human community has ever formed on the Spratly Islands"[336] and that, based on the historic record, all of the economic activity in the Spratly Islands "has been essentially extractive in nature"[337] and that this does not constitute "evidence of an economic life of their own."[338]

On the basis of this evidence, coupled with the above-detailed interpretation of Article 121(3) of the Convention, the Tribunal concluded that none of the above high-tide features in the Spratly Islands,[339] "are capable of sustaining human habitation or an economic life of their own within the meaning of those terms in Article 121(3)" meaning that all of the above high-tide Spratly Islands "are therefore legally rocks for purposes of Article 121(3) and do not generate entitlements to an exclusive economic zone or continental shelf."[340] Scarborough Reef, or as the Tribunal terms the feature "Scarborough Shoal", was similarly determined to be a rock within the meaning of Article 121(3).[341]

333 Ibid., para. 520.
334 Ibid., paras 618–619.
335 Ibid., para. 620.
336 Ibid., para. 621.
337 Ibid., para. 623.
338 Ibid., para. 624.
339 This finding related to Itu Aba, Thitu, West York, Spratly Island, Southwest Cay and Northeast Cay specifically but also to "less significant high-tide features in the Spratly Islands, which are even less capable of sustaining economic life". Ibid., para. 625.
340 Ibid., paras 626 and 646. Here it can be noted that the Tribunal did not examine all of the insular features making up the Spratly Islands individually. However, the larger insular features were examined and smaller above high-tide features are captured by this language. For detailed examination of insular features in the South China Sea featuring satellite image-based mapping see, Centre for International Law (CIL), 'NUS Satellite Research Project on Insular Geographic Features in the South China Sea', available at, https://cil.nus.edu.sg/south-china-sea-satellite-mapping-project/. See also, Lyons et al (n 73) at 146–148 and 153.
341 South China Sea Arbitration, Award (n 3), para. 554.

4 Almost Islands?: Low-tide Elevations and Artificial Islands

The South China Sea is host to myriad features that are submerged at high-tide but partially uncovered at low-tide, that is, low-tide elevations (LTEs). A number of LTEs and small above high-tide islands in the South China Sea have been subject to reclamation and island-building activities. Additionally, entirely and permanently submerged banks and shoals in the region have been subject to contested claims. This section deals with the definition of these features, the maritime entitlements associated with them and the Tribunal's findings in respect of them as well as related activities.

4.1 *Low-tide Elevations*

Article 13 of the LOSC which defines an LTE as a follows:

1. A low-tide elevation is a naturally formed area of land which is surrounded by and above water at low tide but submerged at high tide. Where a low-tide elevation is situated wholly or partly at a distance not exceeding the breadth of the territorial sea from the mainland or an island, the low-water line on that elevation may be used as the baseline for measuring the breadth of the territorial sea.
2. Where a low-tide elevation is wholly situated at a distance exceeding the breadth of the territorial sea from the mainland or an island, it has no territorial sea of its own.[342]

Analogous to the definition of islands under Article 121(1), therefore, LTEs, are required to be "naturally-formed" areas of "land" and "surrounded by water"[343] but are distinguished from the islands on account of their inundated state at high-tide.[344] A key consideration in this context is therefore what level of high-tide should be used. Analogous to the mention to tidal levels in Articles 5 and 121(1), Article 13 of the LOSC is silent as to which vertical datum is the appropriate choice. While LTEs have generally been viewed as marginal and as well as unstable or ephemeral features, they are still of potential significance in

342 LOSC, Article 13. A repetition of Article 11 of the Convention on the Territorial Sea and Contiguous Zone (n 13). Regarding the historical development of the definition of LTEs see, See for example, H Jayewardene, (n 8), at 7. See also, CH Schofield and RN Schofield, 'Testing the Waters: Charting the Evolution of Claims to and from Low-Tide Elevations and Artificial Islands Under the Law of the Sea' (2016) 1 *Asia-Pacific Journal for Ocean Law and Policy* 37–67.

343 LOSC, Articles 13 and 121.

344 R Lavalle, 'Not Quite a Sure Thing: The Maritime Areas of Rocks and Low-tide Elevations Under the UN Law of the Sea Convention' (2004) 19(1) *International Journal of Marine and Coastal Law* 43–69, at 57–64.

advancing maritime jurisdictional claims and their status has, on occasion, led to disputes over their use as basepoints in the context of maritime boundary delimitation.

With respect to sovereignty claims, the submerged state of LTEs during part of the tidal cycle has in the past given rise to uncertainty as to whether such features are truly land territory which can be subject to appropriation, that is, to a claim to sovereignty over it.[345]

However, in its 2012 Judgment in the Territorial and Maritime Dispute case between Nicaragua and Colombia,[346] the ICJ reached a more definitive conclusion. While acknowledging that "[i]t is well established in international law that islands, however small, are capable of appropriation"[347] the Court went on to state explicitly that "[b]y contrast, low-tide elevations cannot be appropriated."[348] The Arbitral Tribunal in the South China Sea case concurred with this ruling.[349]

Although it is now clear that LTEs cannot be appropriated, they may still be under the sovereignty of a coastal State by virtue of falling within maritime zones over which the coastal State has sovereignty, that is, within internal waters, archipelagic waters and the territorial sea.[350] It follows that the coastal State would have respective sovereign rights and exclusive jurisdiction over LTEs located within its EEZ or on its continental shelf.[351]

With respect to maritime entitlements, LTEs generate no territorial sea of their own. However, they may serve as basepoints with respect to generating maritime zone limits and in the construction of maritime boundary lines, if the LTE in question falls "wholly or partly at a distance not exceeding the breadth of the territorial sea from the mainland or an island".[352] The value of LTEs as

345 See, in particular, the Qatar-Bahrain case (n 57), para. 205. See also, Case concerning Sovereignty over Pedra Branca/Pulau Batu Puteh, Middle Rocks and South Ledge (Malaysia/Singapore), ICJ Judgment of 23 May 2008, paras 297 and 299; and, Beckman and Schofield (n 17), at 4.

346 Nicaragua-Colombia case (n 41), paras 191–193.

347 Ibid., para. 26.

348 Ibid.

349 South China Sea Arbitration, Award (n 3), paras 309 and 1043.

350 See, for example, Qatar-Bahrain Case (n 57), para. 204.

351 Lavalle view LTEs beyond territorial sea limits as "legally non-entities". See, R Lavalle, 'The Rights of States over Low-tide Elevations: A Legal Analysis' (2014) 29 *International Journal of Marine and Coastal Law*, 457–479, at 473.

352 LOSC, Article 13(1). However, LTEs falling wholly or partly within a territorial sea limit measured from a straight line type of baseline baseline such as a straight baseline or a river or bay closing line, but not the normal baseline along the coast of a mainland or island, cannot serve as basepoints. The United Nations Group of Technical Experts on Baselines was of the view that if a low-tide elevation falls within the territorial sea

basepoints for generating maritime claims is thus dependant on proximity to above-high tide coasts, leading them to be termed "parasitic" basepoints.[353]

Further, low-tide elevations which fall wholly or partly within the territorial sea of another low-tide elevation (itself wholly or partly within the territorial sea of a mainland or island coast), do not qualify as basepoints for generating maritime claims such that there can be no 'stepping stone' or 'leap frog' type effect between low-tide elevations further and further offshore linked by territorial seas. This scenario is illustrated in Figure 8 where LTE 1 (wholly within 12 M of the mainland/island coast) and LTE 2 (partially within 12 M of the mainland/island coast) qualify as territorial sea basepoints but LTEs 3 and 4 (located wholly seaward of the 12 M territorial sea limit measured from mainland or island coasts) do not, notwithstanding the fact that LTE 3 is within 12 M of LTE 2 and LTE 4 within 12 M of LTE 3.[354]

It follows that LTEs located beyond the territorial sea generate no maritime zones of their own meaning that they represent "no more than a navigation hazard".[355]

The Tribunal in the South China Sea case classified certain features, for example, Mischief Reef and Second Thomas Shoal, as LTEs. Further, as a consequence of its ruling on the Nine-Dash line, coupled with its conclusion that none of the above high-tide features of the Spratly Islands can generate exclusive economic zone or continental shelf rights, the Tribunal concluded that these features are located in an area "not overlapped by the entitlements generated by any maritime feature claimed by China" and that therefore these LTEs "form part of the exclusive economic zone and continental shelf of the Philippines."[356]

Some of China's recent large-scale island-building activities in the South China Sea have occurred on LTEs including Mischief Reef and Second Thomas Shoal. As these features had been determined to be part of the continental shelf of the Philippines, the Tribunal ruled that China, having proceeded in its activities without the permission of the Philippines, had

generated from a bay closing line, rather than the mainland, this "does not bring it within the scope of article 13." See, United Nations (n 63), at 14.

353 Symmons (n 103, 1995), at 7.

354 Schofield and Schofield (n 342), at 63–64.

355 Symmons (n 103, 1995), at 7. LTE's may, however, be used as basepoints for straight baselines if lighthouses or similar structures have been constructed on them or where general international recognition of the drawing of baselines from such features exists. See, LOSC, Article 7(4).

356 South China Sea Arbitration, Award (n 3), para. 647.

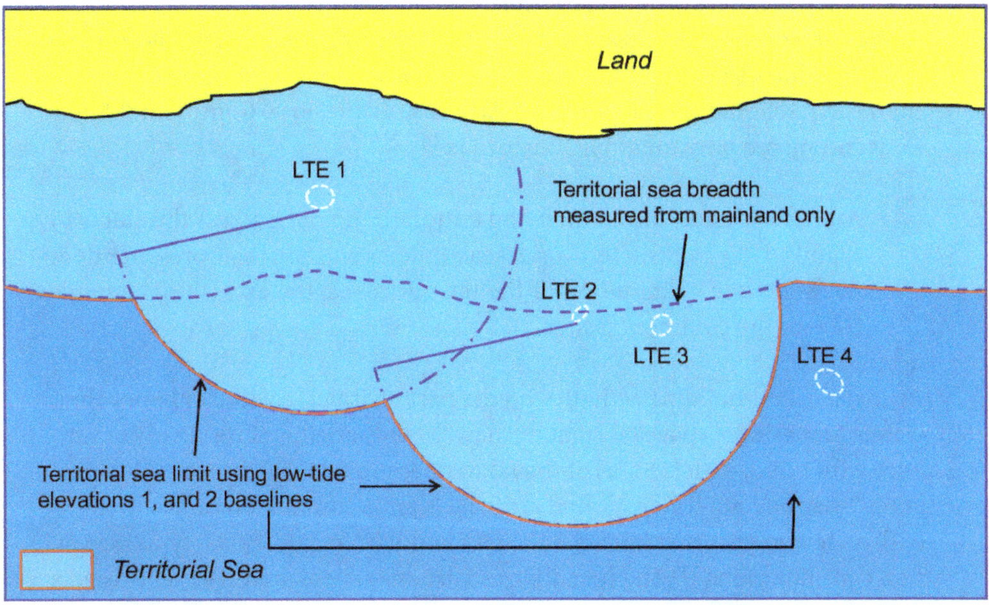

FIGURE 8 The Role of Low-tide Elevations in the Generation of Maritime Limits
SOURCE: ANDI ARSANA AND CLIVE SCHOFIELD[357]

infringed the sovereign rights of the Philippines, breaching Articles 60 and 80 of the Convention.[358]

These findings indicate that while, as noted above, an LTE cannot be converted through artificial intervention into a rock nor a rock into a fully entitled island within the meaning of Article 121 of the LOSC,[359] a feature can nonetheless be changed in character from an LTE to an artificial island or, rather, have artificial structures superimposed on top of it.[360] However, this can only be legally achieved if the LTE in question is located within the coastal State's EEZ or continental shelf.[361]

357 IHO (n 5), Figure 4.4, Chapter 4, 11.
358 Ibid., para. 1043.
359 Ibid., para. 508.
360 Ibid., para. 1037.
361 It can also be noted that LTEs are often ignored as basepoints in the delimitation of maritime boundaries as occurred in the Bay of Bengal. See, Dispute Concerning Delimitation of the Maritime Boundary between Bangladesh and Myanmar in the Bay of Bengal (Bangladesh/Myanmar), International Tribunal for the Law of the Sea (ITLOS), Case no.16, Judgment, 14 March 2012; and Bay of Bengal Maritime Boundary Arbitration between Bangladesh and India (Bangladesh-India), Permanent Court of Arbitration, Final Award of 7 July 2014, available at https://pca-cpa.org/en/cases/18/., para. 261.

4.2 *Artificial Islands, Installations and Structures*

While the status of artificial islands caused considerable debate at an early stage in efforts to codify the international law of the sea,[362] Article 60(8) of the LOSC, echoing the language of Article 5 of the 1958 Continental Shelf, Convention, provides unambiguously that:

> Artificial islands, installation and structures do not possess the status of islands. They have no territorial sea of their own, and their presence does not affect the delimitation of the territorial sea, the exclusive economic zone or the continental shelf.

Artificial island-building activities on the part of States, keen to enhance their claims to maritime space by creating 'new' islands are therefore clearly at variance with LOSC. Article 60(4) of the LOSC does provide that "reasonable safety zones" may be established around artificial islands, installations and structures with a view to ensuring both their safety and with regard to safety of navigation considerations.[363] The breadth of such zones is not, however, to "exceed a distance of 500 metres around them".[364]

The above-mentioned safety zones that may be established around artificial islands, installations and structures are to be measured from "each point of their outer edge" in accordance with Article 60(5) of LOSC. The determination of such zones is to take into account "applicable international standards" and does provide the caveat that such safety zones can be varied if "authorized by generally accepted international standards or as recommended by the competent international organization."[365] Due notice regarding the extent of safety zones is also required.

Concerns have been raised as to whether a 500 m-breadth safety zone is adequate for the purpose of ensuring the safety of valuable offshore installations potentially vulnerable to maritime terrorist incidents.[366] This issue is likely to become more pressing as installations and structures proliferate in the

362 See, for example, Jayewardene (n 8), at 7–8; PC Jessup, *The Law of Territorial Waters and Maritime Jurisdiction*, (G.A, Jennings: New York, N.Y., 1927), 69–70, quoted in ibid., at 7.

363 LOSC, Article 60(4).

364 LOSC, Article 60(5).

365 Ibid.

366 See, for example, M Kashubsky, 'Protecting Offshore Oil and Gas Installations: Security Threats and Countervailing Measures' (August 2013) *Journal of Energy Security* available at, http://www.ensec.org/index.php?option=com_content&view=article&id=453:protecting-offshore-oil-and-gas-installations-security-threats-and-countervailing-measures&catid=137:issue-content&Itemid=422.

marine environment, whether for scientific, ocean energy or marine resource purposes, suggesting that the spatial scope of maritime spaces covered by safety zones is set to substantially increase in the future.[367]

Although artificial islands, installations and structures are not islands and have no maritime zones measured from them save for safety zones, a State may have sovereignty over over such features depending upon where they are constructed. In an analogous fashion to sovereignty over LTEs the coastal State would have sovereignty over artificial islands it has constructed within zones under its own sovereignty, namely within its internal waters, archipelagic waters and the territorial sea.

Within its EEZ the coastal State, in accordance with LOSC Article 60(1), has "the exclusive right to construct and to authorize and regulate the construction, operation and use of" artificial islands, installations and structures although such constructions must be for economic purposes in keeping with the overarching purpose of the EEZ. Article 60 of the LOSC also articulates obligations related to the construction of artificial island, installations and structures including the need to provide "due notice" concerning the construction of such facilities as well as the provision and maintenance of "permanent means for giving warning of their presence" and concerning the removal of disused or abandoned installations and structures in keeping with "generally accepted international standards" established by the competent international organisation.[368] These provisions are also applicable to the continental shelf of the coastal State through Article 80 of the Convention. While all States have the right to construct artificial island, installations and structures on the high seas but detailed rules on such constructions have yet to be articulated.

Artificial islands and island-building activities were a major feature of the South China Sea case. Numerous clamant States have undertaken reclamation and construction activities, generally on the South China Sea islands that they occupy. The Asia Maritime Transparency Initiative (AMTI) has compiled satellite imagery of over 90 "outposts" that have been constructed by the claimant States on in excess of 70 features, "many of which have seen expansion in recent

367 For example, offshore oil and gas infrastructure such as mooring and loading points remote from production platforms as well as the advent of large-scale windfarms the largest of which at the time of writing, Hornsea One, featured 174 wind turbines covering an area of 407 km² with larger developments under construction. See, Orstead, 'Our wind farms', available at https://orsted.co.uk/energy-solutions/offshore-wind; see also, S tho Pesch, 'Coastal State Jurisdiction around Installations: Safety Zones in the Law of the Sea (2015) 30 *International Journal of Marine and Coastal Law* 512–532.

368 LOSC, Article 60(3).

years".[369] Malaysia,[370] the Philippines[371] and Vietnam[372] have all undertaken reclamation activities on features that they occupy. However, the speed and scale of China's island-building activities on seven features that it occupies in the Spratly Islands group in recent years has been of another order of rapidity and magnitude. Indeed, AMTI records that, "since 2013, China has engaged in unprecedented dredging and artificial island-building in the Spratlys, creating 3,200 acres of new land."[373] The area reclaimed equates to 12.95 km^2, a figure that is thrown into sharp relief by estimates that, as noted above, prior to China's large-scale island-building campaign, the largest dozen islands in the Spratly Islands group had a combined land area of less than 2 km^2.[374]

While it is generally accepted that a coastal State is entitled,

> on a natural island to construct harbour works, coast protection works or an airport with runways projecting into the sea, all as bona fide public works, and then to use the low-water mark of these works as baselines.[375]

The Tribunal in the South China Sea made it clear that reclamation activities, including the large-scale island-building and reclamation activities undertaken by China, and to a lesser extent by other States in the South China Sea, cannot convert an LTE into a rock within the meaning of Article 121(3) of the LOSC or transform a such a rock into a fully entitled island.[376]

With respect to the environmental consequences of China's island-building, the Tribunal noted that in addition to the general obligation for parties to the LOSC to "protect and preserve the marine environment",[377] Part XII of the Convention at Article 206 requires that assessments be undertaken when States have "reasonable grounds" for the view that planned activities

369 See, Asia Maritime Transparency Initiative (AMTI) 'Occupation and Island Building' available at https://amti.csis.org/island-tracker/.

370 See, AMTI, 'Malaysia Island Tracker', available at https://amti.csis.org/island-tracker/malaysia/.

371 For example, in relation to the airstrip located on Thitu Island (Pag-asa to the Philippines). See, AMTI, 'Philippines Island Tracker', available at https://amti.csis.org/island-tracker/philippines/.

372 AMTI reports that Vietnam has "reclaimed new land at 8 of the 10 rocks it occupies and built out many of its small outposts on submerged reefs and banks." See, AMTI, 'Vietnam Island Tracker', available at https://amti.csis.org/island-tracker/vietnam/.

373 See, AMTI, 'China Island Tracker', available at https://amti.csis.org/island-tracker/china/.

374 Beckman and Schofield, (n 175), at 210.

375 Anderson (n 7), at 328.

376 South China Sea Arbitration, Award (n 3), para. 508.

377 LOSC, Article 192.

under their jurisdiction or control "may cause substantial pollution of or significant and harmful changes to the marine environment".[378] Under such circumstances there is an obligation on States to "as far as practicable, assess the potential effects of such activities on the marine environment" and, crucially, to "communicate reports of the results of such assessments" in keeping with Article 205 of the LOSC.[379]

Despite multiple claims on the part of Chinese officials of China having conducted "thorough studies", "scientific assessments", and "rigorous tests",[380] the Tribunal found that neither the Tribunal itself, the Tribunal's appointed experts nor those of the Philippines "have been able to identify any report that would resemble an environmental impact assessment that meets the requirements of Article 206 of the Convention" or indeed under China's own domestic legislation relating to EIAs.[381]

While the Tribunal was unable to make a definitive finding that China had or had not prepared an EIA relating to its island-building activities in light of the repeated statements by Chinese officials that it had done so, it deemed that this was not necessary for a breach of Article 206 of the LOSC to have occurred as China was under an obligation to communicate its EIA to competent international organizations (which should make them available to all States) and had not done so despite being directly asked to do so.[382] Accordingly, the Tribunal found that China was in breach of Article 206 of the LOSC since "a State must not only prepare an EIA but also must communicate it".[383]

The Tribunal was explicit in finding that China has caused severe harm to the coral reef environment and violated its obligation to preserve and protect fragile ecosystems and the habitat of depleted, threatened, or endangered species through its recent large-scale land reclamation and construction of artificial islands.[384] The Tribunal was damning in its language, underscoring that China had caused "irreparable harm" such that in practical terms "neither this decision nor any action that either Party may take in response can undo

378 LOSC, Article 206.

379 Ibid. Dealing with the publication of reports, Article 205 states that States shall publish or otherwise make available reports of results obtained pursuant to Article 204 and "make them available to all States." Article 204, in turn, relates to the monitoring of the risks and effects of pollution.

380 As quoted in South China Sea Arbitration, Award (n 3), para. 921.

381 Ibid., para. 989. Specifically, China's Environmental Impact Assessment Law of 2002.

382 Ibid., para. 991.

383 Ibid.

384 In particular, the Tribunal found that China, through its island-building activities, had "breached Articles 192, 194(1), 194(5), 197, 123, and 206 of the Convention." Ibid., para. 993.

the permanent damage that has been done to the coral reef habitats of the South China Sea", and further that China had:

> aggravated the dispute between the Parties with respect to the marine environment at Mischief Reef and extended that dispute to encompass additional features that became the sites of large-scale construction work while this arbitration was ongoing.[385]

Moreover, the Tribunal concluded that "China has undermined the integrity" of the arbitration proceedings and made the Tribunal's task more difficult as it had "permanently destroyed evidence of the natural status" of features in the Spratly Islands at the very time the Tribunal had been tasked to assess the status of those features such that they "are now literally buried under millions of tons of sand and concrete".[386] Here it can be observed that satellite imagery, photographic and video evidence as well as scientific studies, media coverage and expert reports were especially valuable in enabling the Tribunal to rule that China had breached Articles 192 and 194(5) of the LOSC.[387]

4.3 *Submerged Banks and Shoals*

Banks and shoals that are never above low-water have no capacity to generate claims to maritime jurisdiction under LOSC. Furthermore, entirely submerged features have no zone generative capacity even if a structure has been built on them, which is itself permanently above sea level. Despite the clarity of the international law of the sea in this context, States have nonetheless made sovereignty claims to such features.

In the South China Sea context it has also been reported that both China and Taiwan claim the Macclesfield Bank as islands capable of generating maritime claims to jurisdiction.[388] This is despite the fact that the features in question are a submerged atoll and outlying shoals which lie at least nine meters below

385 Ibid., para. 1178.

386 Ibid., para. 1179.

387 Keating (n 83), at 543. The Tribunal also ruled on other environmental issues including harmful fishing practices and the harvesting of endangered species. See, South China Sea Arbitration, Award (n 3), paras 815–851, 912–915, 939–975 and 992. See also, T Stephens, 'The Collateral Damage from China's "Great Wall of Sand" – the Environmental Dimensions of the South China Sea Case' (2017) 17/06 Sydney Law School, Legal Studies Research Paper.

388 See, D Dzurek, *The Spratly Islands: Who's On First?*, Maritime Briefing, 2(1) (International Boundaries Research Unit: Durham, 1996), at 54.

sea level (see Figure 7).[389] Chinese hydrographic sources reinforce the point that this is a submerged feature, record least water depths over Macclesfield Bank of 12–20 m and 9–16 with respect to "submerged cays and reefs" located east of the submerged lagoon of Macclesfield Bank where water depths of 60–80 m are reported.[390]

Chinese sources have referred to Macclesfield Bank and Scarborough Reef collectively as the Zhongsha Islands [Zhongsha Qundao],[391] although the features are approximately 168 M apart and separated by waters over 4,000 m deep. This appears to be a way to obfuscate the reality that China claims an entirely and permanently submerged feature as a part of its territory by associating it with the nearest, albeit tiny and distant insular feature.

While Macclesfield Bank was not considered in the South China Sea case, an analogous submerged bank, Reed Bank, was covered by the Award in that case and was determined to be "an entirely submerged reef formation that cannot give rise to maritime entitlements".[392] This finding underscores what is clear from the provisions of the Convention as well as international law generally, with respect to submerged parts of the sea floor. That is, that such submerged features, such as Macclesfield Bank, are not capable of appropriation and cannot generate any zones of maritime jurisdiction.

5 Reactions to the South China Sea Award

5.1 *International Responses*

The Award of the Arbitral Tribunal in the South China Sea case was greeted in a variety of ways internationally, from clear calls for the parties to respect and implement the Award, to highly critical responses, challenging the Tribunal's jurisdiction to hear the case in the first place as well as criticising its legal reasoning and appraisal of the evidence before it.

---

389 The relevant British Admiralty Pilot states that Macclesfield Bank is a "below-water atoll" with many patches where depths are "less than 20 m" indicates that the shallowest part of Macclesfield Bank has "a depth of 11.9 m". See, United Kingdom Hydrographic Office (UKHO), *Admiralty Sailing Directions: China Sea Pilot (NP30)*, Vol.1, 8th edition (UKHO: Taunton, 2010), at 69.

390 See, Navigation Guarantee Department of the Chinese Navy Headquarters, *China Sailing Directions: South China Sea* (A103) (2011).

391 See, for example, Chinese Society of International Law (CSIL), 'The South China Sea Arbitration Awards: A Critical Study' (2018) 17(2) *Chinese Journal of International Law* 207–748, at 217.

392 South China Sea Arbitration, Award (n 3), para. 1203(A)(3)(c).

According to the Asia Maritime Transparency Initiative (AMTI) which has sought to track reactions to the Award of the Tribunal in the South China Sea case, in total eight countries have publicly called for it to be respected.[393] These include Australia,[394] Canada,[395] Japan,[396] New Zealand,[397] the United Kingdom[398] and the United States.[399] Further, among the South China Sea coastal States the Philippines, rather unsurprisingly, also called on China to abide by the Award of the Tribunal, and Vietnam welcomed the Tribunal's ruling.[400]

393 Asia Maritime Transparency Initiative (AMTI), 'Arbitration support tracker', available at https://amti.csis.org/arbitration-support-tracker/.

394 See Joint Statement by the Foreign Ministers of Australia and Japan together with the Secretary of State of the United States. The Ministers made their joint statement following the seventh ministerial meeting of the Trilateral Strategic Dialogue (TSD) on 7 August 2017, available at https://www.state.gov/r/pa/prs/ps/2017/08/273216.htm, (last accessed 30 July 2020).

395 See, Global Affairs Canada, Statement by Honourable Stéphane Dion, Minister of Foreign Affairs, 'Canadian Statement on South China Sea Arbitration', 21 July 2016, available at https://www.canada.ca/en/global-affairs/news/2016/07/canadian-statement-on-south-china-sea-arbitration.html, (last accessed 30 July 2020).

396 See Joint Statement (n 394). See also, Statement by Foreign Minister Fumio Kishida, 'Arbitration between the Republic of the Philippines and the People's Republic of China regarding the South China Sea (Final Award by the Arbitral Tribunal)', 12 July 2016, available at https://www.mofa.go.jp/press/release/press4e_001204.html, (last accessed 30 July 2020).

397 See, Government of New Zealand, Foreign Minister Murray McCully, 'NZ comment on South China Sea Tribunal ruling', 13 July 2016, available at https://www.beehive.govt.nz/release/nz-comment-south-china-sea-tribunal-ruling?utm_source=feedburner&utm_medium=feed&utm_campaign=Feed%3A+beehive-govt-nz%2Fportfolio%2Fforeign-affairs+%28Foreign+Affairs+-+beehive.govt.nz%29, (last accessed 30 July 2020).

398 Statement by Hon. Mark Field, Minister of State for Asia and the Pacific, United Kingdom Foreign and Commonwealth Office. See, F Mangosing, 'UK, Australia push for respect for rule of law, Hague ruling', Inquirer, 17 August 2018, available at https://globalnation.inquirer.net/169118/uk-australia-push-respect-rule-law-hague-ruling.

399 See, J Kirby, 'Decision in the Philippines-China Arbitration', Press Statement, 12 July 2016, United States Department of State, available at https://2009-2017.state.gov/r/pa/prs/ps/2016/07/259587.htm. The United States Presidential Press Secretary also noted that the Tribunal's ruling is "final and binding." The White House, Press Briefing by Press Secretary Josh Earnest, 13 July 2016, available at https://obamawhitehouse.archives.gov/the-press-office/2016/07/13/press-briefing-press-secretary-josh-earnest-7132016, (last accessed 30 July 2020). See also, J Kraska, 'The Struggle for Law in the South China Sea', paper presented at Seapower and Projection Forces in the South China Sea: Hearing before the Subcommittee on Seapower and Projection Forces of the Committee on Armed Services, House of Representatives, One Hundred Fourteenth Congress, Second Session, Hearing Held 21 September 2016 (U.S. Government Publishing Office: Washington, D.C., 2018) 47–69, at 58.

400 See, 'Remarks of the Spokesperson of the Ministry of Foreign Affairs of Viet Nam on Viet Nam's reaction to the issuance of the Award by the Tribunal constituted under Annex

Other responses have been more guarded. For instance, the Spokesperson for the Secretary-General of the United Nations merely indicated the Secretary-General's awareness of the Award and reiterated his call on all parties to "resolve their disputes in the South China Sea in a peaceful and amicable manner through dialogue and in conformity with international law, including the UN Charter" whilst observing that "the UN doesn't have a position on the legal and procedural merits of the case or on the disputed claims"[401] This non-position on the part of the UN Secretary-General likely reflects his need to adopt a studiously neutral stance and work with all sides, as well as China's position as a permanent member of the United Nations Security Council.

A Joint Communiqué was also issued after the 49th meeting of the Foreign Ministers of the Association of Southeast Asian Nations (ASEAN) in Vientiane, Laos, on 24 July 2016 took a similarly neutral tone, making no direct reference to the Tribunal's Award.[402] However, the Foreign Ministry of the Philippines subsequently issued an information note highlighting the communiqué's affirmation of,

> our shared commitment to maintaining and promoting peace, security and stability in the region, as well as to the peaceful resolution of disputes, **including full respect for legal and diplomatic processes**, without resorting to the threat or use of force, in accordance with the universally recognized principles of international law, including the 1982 United Nations Convention on the Law of the Sea.[403]

According to the Philippines information note, this reflected the "essence of this milestone decision" and "clearly recognizes that the Philippines took in

VII to the United Nations Convention on the Law of the Sea in the arbitration between the Philippines and China', 12 July 2016, available at https://seasresearch.wordpress.com/2016/07/06/remarks-by-vietnams-mofa-spokesperson-on-vietnams-reaction-to-the-final-award-of-the-arbitration-case-initiated-by-the-philippines-against-china-by-the-permanent-court-of-arbitration/, (last accessed 30 July 2020).

401 S Dujarric, 'Remarks by Spokesperson for the U.N. Secretary-General on the South China Sea Arbitration', 12 July 2016, available at https://seasresearch.wordpress.com/2016/07/15/remarks-by-spokesperson-for-the-u-n-secretary-general-on-the-south-china-sea-arbitration/, (last accessed 29 July 2020).

402 ASEAN, 'Joint Communiqué of the 49th ASEAN Foreign Ministers' Meeting', 25 July 2016, available at https://asean.org/joint-communique-of-the-49th-asean-foreign-ministers-meeting/.

403 Republic of the Philippines, Department of Foreign Affairs, 'Information Note on the Significance of the 2016 ASEAN Joint Communiqué in Relation to the Arbitral Tribunal Ruling', 1 August 2016, available at https://www.dfa.gov.ph/newsroom/dfa-releases/10072-information-note-on-the-significance-of-the-2016-asean-joint-communique-in-relation-to-the-arbitral-tribunal-ruling (emphasis in original).

filing the arbitration case."[404] This arguably reads overly substantial meaning into some rather bland diplomatic language. The neutral tone of the ASEAN response is perhaps more indicative of disagreements within ASEAN as to how to respond to the South China Sea ruling, driven by a strong desire on the part of some States not to offend China.

In total AMTI has identified 32 States that have issued generally positive statements noting the verdict of the Arbitral Tribunal in the South China Sea case, but stopping short of calling for the parties to abide by it.[405] Among these States were the then 28 members of the European Union (EU) that had not issued statements of their own but which acceded to an EU Statement representing the position of all members.[406] The EU Statement acknowledged the ruling and called on all parties to "clarify their claims and to pursue them in accordance with international law, including the United Nations Convention on the Law of the Sea", without overtly calling on the parties to respect the Tribunal's Award.[407] It can, however, be noted that the EU issued a strongly-worded Declaration in March 2016 which urged "all claimants to resolve disputes through peaceful means, to clarify the basis of their claims, and to pursue them in accordance with international law including UNCLOS *and it arbitration procedures*."[408] A further eight States, Algeria, Brunei, Cambodia, Indonesia, Laos, Serbia, Syria and Thailand, were identified

404 Ibid.

405 These States are Belgium, Bosnia and Hercegovina, Bulgaria, Croatia, Cyprus, Czech Republic, Denmark, Estonia, Finland, France, Germany, Greece, Hungary, Ireland, India, Italy, Latvia, Lithuania, Luxembourg, Malaysia, Malta, Myanmar, The Netherlands, Poland, Portugal, Romania, Singapore, Slovakia, Slovenia, Republic of Korea, Spain and Sweden. See, AMTI (n 393).

406 Ibid; and, European Union (EU), Declaration on the award rendered in the arbitration between the Philippines and China, 15 July 2016, available online, https://eeas.europa.eu/delegations/ cuba/6873/declaration-on-the-award-rendered-in-the-arbitration-between-the-philippines-and-c hina_fr.

407 See, EU, ibid. See also, T Fallon, 'The EU, the South China Sea and China's Successful Wedge Strategy', 13 October 2016, AMTI, available at, https://amti.csis.org/eu-south-china-sea-chinas-successful-wedge-strategy/; and Reuters, 'EU's statement on the South China Sea reflects divisions', *Reuters*, 15 July 2016, available at, https://www.reuters.com/article/southchinasea-ruling-eu/eus-statement-on-south-china-sea-reflects-divisions-idUSL8N1A130Y.

408 See, EU, Declaration by the high representative on behalf of the EU on recent developments in the South China Sea, 11 March 2016, available online, https://www. consilium.europa.eu/en/press/press-releases/2016/03/11/hr-declaration-on-bealf-of-eu-recent-de velopments-south-china-sea/ (emphasis added).

as having made more muted or neutral statements about the South China Sea without addressing the ruling.[409]

Unsurprisingly, China itself condemned the Award in forthright terms through a statement of the Ministry of Foreign Affairs that China "neither accepts nor recognizes" the Award and solemnly declaring it to be "null and void" and of "no binding force."[410] This statement reiterated China's positions that the Tribunal lacked jurisdiction, that the arbitration was unilaterally initiated by the Philippines in bad faith not to resolve disputes between China and the Philippines, "but to deny China's territorial sovereignty and maritime rights and interests in the South China Sea."[411]

The statement asserted that the arbitration "violates international law" by addressing issues concerning territorial sovereignty which therefore "inevitably concerns and cannot be separated from maritime delimitation between China and the Philippines", pointing out that territorial concerns were not subject to the LOSC and maritime delimitation disputes were excluded from compulsory dispute resolution under the Convention in keeping with China's 2006 Declaration.[412] China's statement went on to indicate that the arbitration also violated international law because it violated bilateral agreement between China and the Philippines to settle their disputes concerning the South China Sea through negotiations and further by violating a commitment on the part of China and the ASEAN member States including the Philippines under the 2002 Declaration on the Code of conduct of Parties in the South China Sea to resolve disputes through negotiations.[413]

While this statement was broad in scope and did not directly address the issue of Article 121 it argued that the arbitration "selectively takes relevant islands and reefs out of the macro-geographical framework" of the South China Sea Islands and "subjectively and speculatively interprets and applies" the LOSC and "obviously errs in ascertaining facts and applying the law."[414]

Five other States – Montenegro, Pakistan, Russia, Sudan and Vanuatu – publically rejected the Tribunal's award.[415] It can be noted that these States that have publically rejected the Award are either generally hostile to international

409 See, AMTI (n 393).
410 China, Statement of the Ministry of Foreign Affairs (n 165).
411 Ibid.
412 Ibid.; and UNTC (n 163).
413 Ibid.
414 Ibid.
415 See ibid.

litigation[416] or have close bilateral political and economic relationships with China.[417]

It can also be observed that this is rather less than had been claimed by the Chinese Ministry of Foreign Affairs just prior to the ruling which asserted that more than 60 States agreed with China's position that the Tribunal lacked jurisdiction and its Award was therefore invalid.[418] Additionally, and again unsurprisingly, Taiwan, which largely shares mainland China's position regarding the South China Sea disputes and which occupies the largest feature in the Spratly Islands, Itu Aba (referred to by Taiwan authorities as Taiping Dao), likewise rejected the Tribunal's ruling as "completely unacceptable to the Government of the Republic of China."[419]

The relatively muted international response to the Award has been characterised as "generally lukewarm" and attributed to "very activist Chinese diplomacy warning other countries against open support" for the ruling, backed by China's powerful economic leverage.[420] Indeed, it has been reported that the it took three days of "protracted negotiations" to produce the abovementioned EU statement due to disagreements over the strength of the language to be used.[421] In this context, while Croatia has had a negative experience with an arbitration process at the PCA in recent years which may explain its position with respect to the South China Sea arbitration, it has been noted

416 This observation is arguably borne out by the Russian Federation's refusal to participate in the Arctic Sunrise case. See, Arctic Sunrise Arbitration (Netherlands v. Russia), Case No. 2014–02, Award on the Merits. See also, for example, AG Oude Elferink, 'The Russian Federation and the Arctic Sunrise Case: Hot Pursuit and Other Issues under the LOSC' (2016) 92 *International Legal Studies*, 381–406.

417 For example, China is financing the Bar-Boljare highway, the largest construction project in Montenegro's history, has long-standing partnerships with both Pakistan, including multi-billion dollar investments related to the China-Pakistan Economic Corridor, and Sudan, especially around oil resources and provides substantial development aid to Vanuatu.

418 AMTI (n 393).

419 S Tiezzi, 'Taiwan: South China Sea Ruling "Completely Unacceptable"', *The Diplomat*, 13 July 2016, available at https://thediplomat.com/2016/07/taiwan-south-china-sea-ruling-completely-unacceptable/. See also, H Lu and E Hou, 'Taiwan does not accept South China Sea ruling: President's Office', Focus Taiwan, CAN English News, 12 July 2016, available at https://focustaiwan.tw/politics/201607120024; N Klein, 'Islands and Rocks after the South China Sea Arbitration',34 (2016) *The Australian Yearbook of International Law* 21–29, at 26.

420 F Zhang, 'Assessing China's response to the South China Sea arbitration ruling' (2017) 71(4) *Australian Journal of International Affairs* 440–459, at 446.

421 See, *Reuters* (n 407).

that both Hungary and Greece are reliant on Chinese investment to facilitate large infrastructure projects.[422]

There seems little doubt that China has engaged in a concerted effort to undermine the legitimacy of the Tribunal. In light of the diplomatic pressure and economic leverage that China is able to bring to bear to help suppress international support for the Award the relatively lacklustre pronouncements of global and regional bodies as well as those of individual States is understandable. Indeed, given the pressure that China has applied in order to dampen the international response to the Tribunal's Award and encourage rejection of it, it is perhaps surprising that the Award received even the moderate support that it did and that the number of States rejecting its findings was limited. More recent international diplomatic correspondence has, however, occurred both referring to and clearly replying on the Tribunal's Award (see Part VI).

5.2 *Scholarly Views*

The Tribunal's Award has sparked a fresh wave, a near tsunami even, of scholarship devoted to the regime of islands and, in particular, the Tribunal's interpretation of it. Consequently, this section of the article does not set out to provide a comprehensive review but instead to offer an indication of the contours of the academic debate. To suggest that the reaction of commentators to the South China Sea Tribunal's Award has been mixed is something of an understatement. A number of publicists welcomed the Award's findings related to the interpretation of the regime of islands.[423] Other commentators were more critical of the Award's findings related to islands. This section of the

422 For example, including the reported plan for China to invest "over half a billion euros in the Greek Port of Piraeus." See, G Gotev, 'EU unable to adopt statement upholding South China Sea ruling', *Euractiv*, 14 July 2016, available at https://www.euractiv.com/section/global-europe/news/eu-unable-to-adopt-statement-upholding-south-china-sea-ruling/.

423 See, for example, American Society of International Law (ASIL), 'Remarks by David Freestone' and 'Remarks by Douglas Guilfoyle', in ASIL, 'The Regime of Islands in the Aftermath of the South China Sea Arbitration', ASIL 2017 Conference panel *Proceedings of the Annual ASIL Meeting* 112 (Cambridge University Press: Cambridge, 2018), 4–7 and 7–10.; T Davenport, 'Legal Implications of the South China Sea Award for Maritime Southeast Asia' (2016) 34 *Australian Yearbook of International Law* 65–86; Gullett (n 126); J-L Hebert, 'The South China Sea Arbitration Award and Its Widespread Implications' (2018) 19(1), *Oregon Review of International Law* 289–314; Keating (n 83), Kraska (n 399), Murphy (n 85); N Oral, '"Rocks" or "Islands"?: Sailing Towards Legal Clarity in the Turbulent South China Sea', Symposium on the South China Sea Arbitration, (2017) 110 *AJIL Unbound*, 279–284; BH Oxman, 'The South China Sea Arbitration Award', University of Miami Legal Studies Research Paper No. 16–41 6 September 2016), available at SSRN, https://ssrn.com/abstract=2835534 or http://dx.doi.org/10.2139/ssrn.2835534 (noting that Oxman served as Counsel for the Philippines in the South China Sea Tribunal but here was commenting as

study concentrates on some of the key issues raised in the latter critiques of the South China Sea Tribunal's Award on the definition of islands. The contributions of Chinese scholars, which tend to be hostile to the Tribunal's Award are touched on separately as they are arguably shaped and constrained by national perspectives and policies.

5.2.1 The term "Rock"

Some commentators have criticised the Tribunal for departing from the objective meaning of the term "rock".[424] As the Tribunal relied on an ordinary definition of the term "rock" by reference to a dictionary,[425] rather than one based a geological understanding of the term,.[426] However, as noted above, the Tribunal took the view that "imposing a geological criteria" on Article 121(3) would lead to "an absurd result."[427] That is, that introducing a "geological qualification" to Article 121(3) of the LOSC would mean that more obviously 'rocky' features would be captured by the provision but that smaller and more insubstantial and potentially less persistent features composed of, for example, sand, silt or mud, would escape the limitation of the provision and generate full EEZ and continental shelf entitlements. The Tribunal's view was that this would defeat the purpose of the provision is persuasive.[428]

Further, with respect to terminology, the Tribunal's classification of insular features into a hierarchy, that is, fully entitled islands, rocks, low-tide elevations and submerged features does not appear, at first glance, to be especially controversial, yet this aspect of the Tribunal's ruling has nonetheless attracted criticism.[429] Objections to the Tribunal's categorisation of insular features stem from the view that Article 121(3) "rocks" should not be considered as a

---

a publicist); and, S Sweeney, 'Rocks v. Islands: Natural Tensions over Artificial Features in the South China Sea' (2017) 31 *Temple International & Comparative Law Journal* 599–634.

424 See, for example, See, Franckx (n 18), at 154–175; AG Oude Elferink, 'The South China Sea Arbitration's Interpretation of Article 121(3) of the LOSC: A Disquieting First' *The JCLOS Blog*, 7 September 2016, available at file:///G:/My%20Drive/Research%20materials/South%20China%20Sea/The-South-China-Sea-Arbitrations-Interpretation-of-Article-1213-of-the-LOSC-A-Disquieting-First.pdf, at 2–3; and S Talmon, 'Regime of Islands', in A Proelss (ed.), *United Nations on the Law of the Sea: A Commentary* (C.H. Beck/Hart/Nomos: Munich/Oxford/Baden-Baden, 2017) 858–880., at 868.

425 Specifically, *The Oxford English Dictionary*. Ibid., para. 480.

426 It can be noted in this context that geological definitions of the term "rock", and in particular the "rock cycle", are dynamic in character. See, for example, National Geographic, 'The Rock Cycle', available at, https://www.nationalgeographic.org/encyclopedia/rock-cycle/.

427 South China Sea Arbitration, Award (n 3) para. 481.

428 Ibid.

429 MH Nordquist, 'UNCLOS Article 121 and Itu Aba in the South China Sea Award: A correct interpretation?', in Jayakumar et al (n 18), 176–204, at 189.

distinct category but only as a narrowly limited exception to a situation where above high-tide insular features are presumed to fully entitled islands.[430]

5.2.2 Does Size Matter?

While the drafting history of the article are replete with proposals regarding a size criterion to distinguish between fully entitled islands and rocks (see Section 2 above), ultimately the drafters of Article 121(3) omitted a reference to size. Thus, it is irrelevant how small, or indeed how large, an Article 121(3) "rock" may be. Nonetheless, the Tribunal's finding that the size of an insular feature was not dispositive has been subject to criticism.[431] The driver for this was that objective definitions of the term "rock" tend to include some consideration of size.[432] The rejection of a size criterion by the drafters of Article 121(3) in large part stemmed from the arbitrary character of any choice size limitation,[433] so these lingering concern over the role of the size of insular features in determining their status is somewhat puzzling. Ultimately, therefore size only retains a residual role in that the area of a feature necessarily provides the space for human habitation or an economic life to occur.[434]

5.2.3 Natural State

A key finding of the Tribunal was that insular status should be based on a particular feature's natural state prior to human intervention and, coupled with this, that historical evidence was likely to be of most value in this context. This has been criticised on the basis the Tribunal of essentially imported the reference to "naturally formed" at Article 121(1) into Article 121(3) and thus rewriting the provision.[435] However, the Tribunal's interpretation on this point was founded on its view that the status of a feature cannot be changed through human intervention. That is, an LTE cannot be built up and transformed into a rock and likewise a rock cannot be converted into a fully entitled island. Against the backdrop of China's large-scale island building efforts, both before and during the arbitral proceedings, which involved the comprehensive destruction or alteration to the physical realities of certain insular features in

430 Ibid., at 190. In keeping with this expansive view of the entitlements to be accorded to features, as opposed to the Tribunal's view of Article 121(3) as a provision of limitation, Nordquist took exception to the Tribunal's finding that Itu Aba was not a fully entitled island. Ibid., at 195–202.

431 South China Sea Arbitration, Award, (n 3), at para. 538.

432 Oude Elferink (n 424), at 3.

433 As the as author himself notes. Ibid., at 5.

434 South China Sea Arbitration, Award (n 3) para. 542.

435 See, for example, Talmon (n 424), at 868; and Nordquist (n 429), at 186.

the South China Sea, historical evidence of the previous condition of features in question appears to be the only viable option. It can also be noted concerning criticisms of the Tribunal's findings on the basis that it essentially rewrote provisions of the Convention appear to deny the potential for the progressive clarification in the interpretation of the regime of islands through judicial decisions such as that of the Tribunal (see Section 6).

5.2.4 Historical Evidence

With respect to the role of historical evidence in determining island status it has been noted that the Tribunal provided no guidance concerning "what temporal limitation, if any, there is on the use of historical evidence to assess the natural capacity of a maritime feature."[436] With respect to this concern, the Tribunal shied away from providing what would inevitably be an arbitrary time limit or date. It can, however, be noted that the Tribunal did indicate that contemporary observations were preferable.[437] In the face of the wholesale changes in the physical characteristics of certain insular features as a consequence of China's large-scale island building operations, and thus the destruction of evidence of the natural condition of these features, the Tribunal was, however, forced to resort to the use of the best available historic evidence, while observing that evidence of this type was not necessarily inferior to contemporary observations so long as it came from a reputable source.[438]

Further considerations on historic aspects of the Tribunal's interpretation also led to the concern that the Tribunal's interpretation was "essentially static" in character with the assessment of insular features "fixed at a certain moment in the past."[439] The concern here was that the capacity of a feature to sustain human habitation or economic life of its own has the potential to change or evolve over time, for instance as a result of climate change.[440] However, the Tribunal's Award does not rule out natural changes that may lead to a feature changing status and is therefore not as locked into a particular point in time as it has been suggested. The Tribunal's reliance on what have been termed "vintage" geospatial information such as charts and sailing directions,[441] some over a century and a half old, in order to determine above

436 See, Oral (n 423), at 281.

437 See, South China Sea Arbitration, Award (n 3), para. 354. See also, Murphy (n 85), at 54.

438 South China Sea Arbitration, Award (n 3), para. 327.

439 Y Tanaka, 'Reflections on the interpretation and Application of Article 121(3) in the South China Sea Arbitration (Merits)' (2017) 48(3–4) *Ocean Development and International Law* 365–385, at 368.

440 Ibid., at 368–369 and 379.

441 Keating (n 83), at 537.

high-tide status has been critiqued on the grounds that this does not take into account significant global mean sea level rise.[442] While there is considerable merit in this argument, the fact that substantial island building activities had served to fundamentally transform a number of insular features in the South China Sea and destroy evidence of their natural condition meant that the Tribunal had little choice but to exercise their judicial discretion and rely on historical evidence as being the most convincing available.

5.2.5 Human Habitation and Economic Life

A number of commentators also found the Tribunal's entwining of human habitation and economic life problematic.[443] However, such criticisms generally fail to explain how economic life might exist without humans and, in any case, the Tribunal did not close the door to the existence of human habitation existing in the absence of economic life or vice-versa.[444] The view that the qualitative element to human habitation introduced through the Tribunal's definition will "raise more questions than it answers" is well made, but arguably addressed by the scope for flexibility in interpretation build into the Tribunal's Award (see below).[445]

The Tribunal's determination that features disproportionately dependent on external support also drew adverse comment.[446] Here commentators perhaps overstate the Tribunal's findings. Indeed, the Tribunal did not entirely prohibit trade or links between an island and supply from exterior sources, but instead emphasised that "relying *predominantly* on the infusion of outside resources" and the "continued injection of external resources"[447] as indicators that a feature does not sustain an economic life of its own. Here there is a degree of interpretational flexibility to allow for the consideration of borderline cases.

5.2.6 Consistency with Past Jurisprudence

It has also been suggested that the South China Sea Arbitral Tribunal's interpretation of the regime of islands is inconsistent with both international and

442 Lyons et al (n 73), at 133. See also, IPCC (n 98).
443 See, for example, Franckx (n 18), at 168–174; Nordquist (n 429), at 187–188; Oude Elferink (n 424) at 2 and 5; and Talmon (n 424), at 872.
444 South China Sea Arbitration, Award (n 3), para. 497.
445 Talmon (n 424), at 877.
446 See, for example, Nordquist (n 429), at 188.
447 South China Sea Arbitration, Award (n 3), para. 500 (emphasis added).

certain domestic judicial decisions.[448] However, as noted above, prior to the South China Sea case international courts and tribunals proved to be adept at side-stepping the challenge of interpreting Article 121 of the LOSC so there is limited international jurisprudence to support this view. For example, while Jan Mayen Island was accorded weight in the delimitation of a continental shelf and fishing zone boundary in the case between Norway and Denmark (Greenland), the ICJ did not address the issue of the insular status of Jan Mayen because Denmark, while employing the terminology of Article 121 of the LOSC, did not argue that Jan Mayen has no entitlement to continental shelf or fishery zones, merely that it should be accorded partial effect in maritime delimitation.[449] The Conciliation Commission tasked with providing recommendations to the governments of Iceland and Norway with respect to the continental shelf area between Iceland and Jan Mayen considered Jan Mayen's status with respect to Article 121 of the LOSC reaching the view that it "must be considered an island" and thus "entitled to a territorial sea, an economic zone and a continental shelf".[450] However, by its nature the decision of the Commission was non-binding in character and the Commission was also arguably mindful of the positions of the parties. Similarly, it has been noted that ITLOS considered Australia's Heard Island, "to be an island" despite its inhospitable, uninhabited and "virtually uninhabitable" nature.[451] The counterpoint here is that the cases in question were focussed on fisheries issues and the parties to these cases did not challenge the existence of EEZ claims around the islands concerned though the Declarations of Judge Vukas are of particular note here as discussed above. Domestic judicial decisions have, predictably enough, reached views consistent with national jurisdictional claims, that is insular possessions of their own country are fully entitled islands.[452]

5.2.7 State Practice

As noted above, there is a considerable gap between much of State practice and the standard established by the Tribunal in the South China Sea case for

448 See in particular, S Talmon, 'The South China Sea Arbitration and the Finality of "Final" Awards' (2017) 8 *Journal of International Dispute* Settlement, 388–401, at 397–398.

449 Jan Mayen case (n 120), para. 80.

450 Report and Recommendations to the Governments of Iceland and Norway of the Conciliation Commission on the Continental Shelf Area Between Iceland and Jan Mayen, June 1981 (1981) ILM 797–842, at 803–804.

451 Talmon (n 448), at 398.

452 Notably the decision of the Norwegian Supreme Court with respect to Abeløya (Abel Island) and the US District Court for the District of Guam concerning Howland and Baker Islands. See, ibid., at 397.

fully entitled island status, and a number of commentators have raised this issue as a source of concern.[453] State practice is not, however, entirely uniform as illustrated above with respect to Roca Alijos, Rockall and Shag Rocks.

While the Tribunal was cognisant of the existence of State practice contrary to its own interpretation of the regime of islands, it was dismissive as to the existence of agreement concerning interpretation of Article 121 based on subsequent State practice. The Tribunal noted that the threshold for accepting such an agreement "is quite high" and, found explicitly that "there is no evidence for an agreement based upon State practice on the interpretation of Article 121(3) which differs from the interpretation of the Tribunal."[454]

That the Tribunal's findings are at odds with excessive State practice does not seem to be a wholly compelling argument against the Award. An analogy can perhaps be drawn to State practice with respect to straight baselines claims. Much of State practice concerning straight baselines is excessive in character, precisely because of ambiguities in the relevant provisions of the LOSC contained in Article 7 that are arguably analogous to those of Article 121(3). Nonetheless, international courts and tribunals have routinely ignored straight baselines in the context of maritime boundary delimitation cases. Further, the ICJ, in the context of the Qatar-Bahrain case, showed little compunction in discounting this arguably excessive State practice in stating unequivocally that the definition of straight baselines is "an exception to the normal rules for the determination of baselines" and "must be applied restrictively",[455] taking no notice of a substantial body of contrary, and largely excessive, State practice.

Nonetheless, it seems highly likely, on the basis of their own national interests, that coastal States will be reluctant to alter their practice, roll back their maritime claims and thereby lose rights over valuable marine resources within these zones. Critical appraisals to the Tribunal's reasoning and findings on this issue have also included arguments as to the exceptionalism of the South China Sea together with observations that the South China Sea Arbitral Tribunal's Award is binding solely on the parties to that case.[456]

---

453 See, 'Remarks by Oliver Lewis' and 'Remarks by Joanna Mossop', ASIL (n 423 10–12 and 12–14; Tanaka (n 439, at 379); J Mossop, 'The South China Sea Arbitration and New Zealand's Maritime Claims' (2017) 15(2) *New Zealand Journal of Public International Law* 265–292; Klein (n 419); L McDermott, 'Philippines v China – Rocks or Islands under International Law' (2017) 36(1) *University of Tasmania Law Review* 36–68., at 67; Nordquist (n 429), at 188; and, YH Song, 'The July 2016 Arbitration Award, Interpretation of Article 121(3) of the UNCLOS, and Selecting Examples of Inconsistent State Practices' (2018) 49 *Ocean Development and International Law* 247–261, at 256.

454 South China Sea Arbitration, Award (n 3), paras 552–553.

455 Qatar-Bahrain Case (n 57), para 212.

456 See, for example, Mossop (n 453 at 280).

Commentators have also pointed to the fact that 200 M limits from certain insular features have been delineated for in excess of four decades without protest from other States suggesting that this may amount to acquiescence on the part of other States to those claims.[457] Here it can be observed that mutual self-interest is likely at work between coastal States with respect to sweeping maritime claims advanced from peripheral insular features. This is, States have been reluctant to protest the expansive claims of other States for fear of their own claims being subject to criticism. It is also questionable whether international protests will be generated unless a coastal State's direct interests are implicated. Thus, there are abundant protests where extensive maritime claims are made from insignificant insular features which result in overlapping maritime claims with neighbouring States. Moreover, potentially problematic insular features are often dealt with by being accorded reduced or no effect in the context of a maritime boundary delimitation. With respect to the unilateral claims of States which serve to reduce the extent of the high seas and the Area, that is, the 'Global Commons', protests are unlikely to be forthcoming. After all the 'Global Commons' itself is not well placed to protest excessive unilateral claims of coastal States and nor are the least developed States with greatest direct interest in deriving benefit from the Global Commons. Further, high seas freedoms such as navigation and the right to lay submarine pipelines and cables through another State's EEZ and continental shelf are preserved, within the EEZ so key third State rights are not impaired by such claims.

Nonetheless, it has been suggested that one of the "less desirable consequences" of the uncertainty over the interpretation of Article 121(3) was that a rock's EEZ and continental shelf claim "however uninhabitable or small that rock might be, might find legitimacy for its claim with the passing of time, through acquiescence or estoppel" if unchallenged.[458] Further, the gulf between the Tribunal's standard for a fully entitled island and State practice led McDorman to caution that LOSC, Article 121(3) is "a provision of deliberately negotiated vagueness" meaning that the Tribunal's detailed interpretation of it "can be viewed perhaps as 'missionary' work" and that "[i]t will be future tribunals, courts and state practice that will determine whether this 'missionary' aspect of the Award finds favour."[459]

---

457 Ibid., at 283–284 and 288.

458 Jesus (n 148), at 586.

459 T McDorman, 'The South China Sea Arbitration', American Society of International Law, *Insights*, 20(17), 18 November 2016, available at https://www.asil.org/insights/volume/20/issue/17/south-china-sea-arbitration.

5.2.8 Artificial Islands and Island-building Activities

China's islands-building activities also provoked scholarly discussion.[460] For example, the Tribunal has been criticised for allowing for 12 M territorial seas around what have been termed are "man-made islands", arguing that this "manufactured maritime territory" was "still a windfall" and not one intended by the LOSC.[461] Given the Tribunal's strong emphasis on assessing the status of features in their natural state prior to human intervention, coupled with the fact that it is now well established that an above high-tide naturally formed insular feature will generate a 12 M breadth territorial sea regardless of its size or composition, this view seems misplaced. Similarly, concerns have been raised that the Tribunal provided "conflicting interpretations of artificial islands", added "complexity to the issue" and an "illogical" approach by at one point determining Mischief Reef to be a low-tide elevation and subsequently finding that China was in breach of its LOSC obligations because it is operating an artificial island there.[462] However, this view seems to miss the point that the Tribunal found that Mischief Reef in its natural state was an LTE but has been transformed into an artificial island, or, alternatively, had one superimposed on it, through China's intervention and illegally so at that since Mischief Reef was determined to be part of the EEZ of the Philippines.

5.2.9 Chinese Views

Commentary on the part of Chinese scholars has been, unsurprisingly, resolutely negative. A prominent example is provided by the Chinese Society of International Law's (CSIL) lengthy[463] assessment of the Award which takes issue with virtually every aspect of the Tribunal's reasoning.[464] In particular, Chapter Five of the CSIL study was the Status of China's Nansha Qundao [Spratly Islands] and Zhongsha Qundao [Macclesfield Bank Islands]. Prior to

460 See, for example, Sweeney (n 423); AW Kohl, 'China's Artificial Island Building Campaign in the South China Sea: Implications for the Reform of the Law of the Sea' (2018) 122 *Dickinson Law Review* 917–937, at 835–936. See also, Saunders who examines whether artificial islands may be considered to be territory under international law, albeit territory not generating a territorial sea. See, I Saunders, 'Artificial Islands and Territory in International Law' (2019) 52 *Vanderbilt Journal of International Law* 643–684.

461 Sweeney (n 423), at 626.

462 Kohl (n 460), at 835–936.

463 At 541 pages long the CSIL paper is 60 pages longer than the South China Sea Award itself. See, CSIL (n 391)

464 Ibid. Following an introductory chapter, the CSIL study addresses jurisdictional issues (326 pages), admissibility concerns (51 pages), historic rights (112 pages), the status of insular features (187 pages), the legality of China's activities in the South China Sea (157 pages) and due process and evidence (90 pages).

addressing the Tribunal's interpretation of Article 121(3) the CSIL study devotes considerable effort to China's claims that the South China Sea islands should be considered together[465] and that the Spratly Islands are an "outlying archipelago of China"[466]

With respect to the above high-tide features in question, if indeed China had uncontested sovereignty over them they would necessarily be dependant mid-ocean archipelagos of a mainland continental State. There is no provision in the LOSC for baselines around such groups of islands, in distinction to islands forming part of an archipelagic State or a fringe of islands along the coast providing a basis for the application of straight baselines.[467] The argument that the application of archipelagic baselines to the dependant archipelagos of continental States because the LOSC does not specifically forbid it seems to be a wilful misreading of the object and purpose of Part IV of the Convention which was specifically designed for archipelagic States which Article 46 of the LOSC provides are those States which are comprised exclusively of "islands or parts of islands" and "constituted wholly by one or more archipelagos and may include other islands", which would seem to clearly exclude continental States such as China from defining archipelagic baselines in accordance with Article 47 of the Convention.

Such arguments also apparently discount the fact that the issue of continental States in possession of coastal or dependant archipelagos was discussed in the course of UNCLOS III. A number of mainland coastal States did argue that the special rules applicable to archipelagos should also be applicable to their offshore island possessions, yet these proposals did not prove successful.[468] Indeed, China was a party to these discussions, arguing for recognition of a particular regime applicable to archipelagic States.[469] Reference to the practice of a coastal States that have defined straight baselines in respect of dependant archipelagos is also hardly convincing since they have been largely

465 Ibid., at 544–556.

466 Ibid., at 557–613. It can be observed that this is a favoured line of criticism of the Tribunal's Award by Chinese authors in particular. For a critique of a number of these contributions see, JA Roach, 'Offshore Archipelagos Enclosed by Straight Baselines: An Excessive Claim?' (2018) 49 *Ocean Development and International Law* 176–202, at 183–187.

467 See, Articles 46–47 and 7(1) of the LOSC respectively.

468 See Jayewardene, (n 8), at 140–142 and MB Tsamenyi, CH Schofield and B Milligan, 'Navigation through Archipelagos: Current State Practice', in MH Nordquist, TB Koh, and JN Moore (eds), *Freedom of the Seas, Passage Rights and the 1982 Law of the Sea Convention* (Martinus Nijhoff: Leiden/Boston, 2009) 413–454.

469 Nandan and Rosenne (n 16), Volume II, at 412–413.

subject to international protests.[470] Moreover, views that contemporary evidence is not used,[471] ignore the fact that China, through its recent large-scale artificial island building efforts, has comprehensively altered and destroyed evidence of the status of features in their natural state.

The Tribunal did, in fact, consider the possibility that China's references to consideration of the Spratly Islands as a whole might signify an assertion on the part of China that the Spratly Islands should be enclosed within a system of archipelagic or straight baselines and therefore be considered as a single unit,[472] The Tribunal specifically ruled out such possibilities.[473] With respect to archipelagic baselines the Tribunal reasoned that their use "is strictly controlled" and "limited" by the Convention to archipelagic States in keeping with Article 46 of the LOSC (see above).[474] As such the Tribunal was explicit in stating that China is "constituted principally by territory on the mainland of Asia and cannot meet the definition of an archipelagic State."[475]

With respect to the application of straight baselines to the Spratly Islands, the Tribunal acknowledged the practice of some coastal States in applying straight baselines "to offshore archipelagos to approximate the effect of archipelagic baselines" but was of the view that "any application of straight baselines to the Spratly Islands in this fashion would be contrary to the Convention."[476] Moreover, the Tribunal indicated that the application of straight baselines "to offshore archipelagos not meeting the criteria for archipelagic baselines ... would effectively render the conditions in Articles 7 and 47 meaningless."[477] The Tribunal also made the point that despite the practice of some mainland coastal States concerning straight baselines being applied to dependant archipelagos it "sees no evidence that any deviations from this rule have amounted to the formation of a new rule of customary international law that would permit a departure from the express provisions of the Convention."[478]

---

470 See, for example, the United States Department of State *Limits in the Seas* series available at https://2009-2017.state.gov/e/oes/ocns/opa/c16065.htm. See also, JA Roach and RW Smith, *United States Responses to Excessive Maritime Claims*, 3rd edition (Martinus Nijhoff: Leiden, 2012), at 108–115.

471 CSIL (n 391), at 511.

472 South China Sea Arbitration, Award (n 3), para. 573.

473 Ibid. Stating that it "cannot agree" with such options.

474 Ibid.

475 Ibid.

476 Ibid., para. 575.

477 Ibid.

478 Ibid., para. 576. On these issues see also, Roach who is of the view that the Arbitral Tribunal's conclusions on these issues were "fully justified and correct." See Roach (n 466), at 191.

While China has, as yet, not defined archipelagic style or straight baselines around the Spratly islands, it can be observed that the straight baselines that China has defined around other islands in the South China Sea, notably the Paracel Islands, do not conform with the requirements of Article 47. In particular, these baselines would not qualify for archipelagic status under the LOSC because the ratio of water to land in the group would far exceed the 9:1 ratio prescribed in LOSC, Article 47(1).[479]

Concerning Article 121, the CSIL paper makes the critique that the Tribunal "rewrote, in effect, the text of Article 121(3), departing from the intent of the drafters of the Convention as well as State practice.[480] The Tribunal is also criticised for allegedly analysing Article 121(3) in isolation from the rest of the article.[481] Regarding the threshold human habitation and economic life of insular features the CSIL is of the view that the Tribunal turned the issue "upside down" by seeking the positive establishment of such capacity rather than applying an assumption of full island status save for exceptional instances.[482] The Tribunal is further criticised for allegedly distorting the ordinary meaning and context of Article 121 such that it "scrambled its object and purpose".[483] Objections were raised over the Tribunal's assessment of insular features based on their natural capacity for which the CSIL found no basis,[484] the addition of the requirements of "settlement" and "community" in the Tribunal's interpretation of human habitation[485] and the requirement that economic life on a feature should be for a local population,[486] as well as the Tribunal's view that economic life is linked to the presence of humans.[487]

A fundamental complaint in the CSIL paper is that the Tribunal erred in seeking to interpret deliberately ambiguous provisions of the Convention.[488]

479 In its analysis of China's straight baseline claims the U.S. Department of State noted that even if hypothetically the Paracel Islands were an independent archipelagic State, the water to land ration within China's declared baselines "would approximate 26.1:1" thus "far exceeding" the maximum limit of 9:1. See, United States Department of State, Bureau of Oceans and Environmental and Scientific Affairs, 'Straight Baseline Claim: China', *Limits in the Seas, No. 117*, 1996, at 8, available at, http://www.state.gov/documents/organization/57692.pdf.

480 Ibid., at 533–537 and 539–543.

481 Ibid., at 524.

482 Ibid., at 525.

483 Ibid., at 526.

484 Ibid.

485 Ibid., at 528.

486 Ibid., at 531

487 Ibid.

488 Ibid., at 533–537.

The CSIL also pointed out that in their opinion Tribunal did not "faithfully" apply its own findings that a group of islands were collectively capable of providing for human habitation or economic life to the Spratly Islands,[489] failed to take into account China's "relevant materials" and did not give "proper weight" to those that it had, including the Chinese (Taiwan) Society for International Law *amicus curiae* submission.[490] Finally, the CSIL study asserted that Japan's Okinotorishima feature was "not remotely compatible" with the Spratly Islands "archipelagos".[491]

Taiwanese scholars have also been critical of the Award.[492] For example, Gau speculates over what might have been had members of the Tribunal taken up Taiwan's offer of a visit to the feature suggesting that "a doubt lingers" and wonders why Taiwan's *Amicus Curiae* submission did not address the legal issues associated with the interpretation of Article 121(3).[493]

6 Conclusions and Implications

The issue of the definition of islands under the international law of the sea and the conundrum of determining island status under Article 121(3) of the LOSC is one that has entertained or frustrated the law of the sea community for decades. The South China Sea Tribunal's Award is a ground breaking one as it offers the first judicial interpretation of Article 121 of the Convention. This consideration, coupled with the unanimous nature of the Tribunal's decision, lends it substantial authority.

Whereas other international judicial bodies have avoided the interpretation of Article 121(3) of the LOSC, the South China Sea Tribunal did not eschew the challenge. In large part this appears to be because the Tribunal was directly confronted with the issue of determining the status of insular features in a way that past cases were not. The Tribunal was also tasked with addressing South China Sea maritime issues and it appears that the Tribunal's desire to assist in the amelioration of these highly contentious disputes was a strong driver behind Tribunal's willingness to take on issues that other judicial bodies have shied away from.

489 Ibid., at 543–545.

490 Ibid., at 546–550.

491 Ibid., at 550–551.

492 See, for example, Song (n 453) and MS Gau, 'The Sino-Philippine Arbitration on the South China Sea Disputes and the Taiwan' (2016) 9(2) *Journal of East Asia and International Law* 479–496.

493 Gau (n 492), at 496. See also, Gullett (n 126), at 35–36.

The Tribunal's detailed and, in this author's view, well-reasoned Award therefore marks a major advance in our understanding of the regime of islands and a significant step forward in the interpretation of the international law of the sea. That said, uncertainties remain and debates over insular status will inevitably persist.

6.1 *Setting a High Standard*

As is widely acknowledged in the literature following the Award, the Tribunal in the South China Sea case clearly set a 'high bar' or threshold for fully entitled island status. This finding is also in distinct contrast to much State practice, something that has excited much comment in the scholarly literature (see below). Here the Tribunal's Award was fundamentally informed by its view that Article 121(3) was designed by the drafters as a provision of limitation with objective of preventing huge windfall gains in terms of maritime entitlements for coastal States in possession of tiny uninhabitable insular features. Further, the Tribunal viewed Article 121(3) as being inextricably linked to the adoption of the EEZ at UNCLOS III, meaning that broad maritime entitlements were to be viewed as being connected to the needs of coastal populations. Indeed, the Tribunal clearly articulated that the object and purpose of the regime of islands was to benefit coastal populations with the Article 121(3) provision being included in order to "disable tiny features from unfairly and inequitably generating enormous entitlements to maritime space that would not serve to benefit the local population."[494] Consequently, the Tribunal was conscious of the need, in its view, to forestall expansive claims from features built up or altered expressly for the purpose of advancing such claims. This reasoning is compelling.

Admittedly with the benefit of hindsight, this interpretation of Article 121 arguably should not come as a complete surprise. For example, there has been a clear trend in international jurisprudence towards awarding small and often remote or uninhabited islands a reduced, often nil, effect in maritime boundary delimitation, especially where the location of such features leads to pronounced and therefore inequitable impacts in the application of equidistance lines.[495] Additionally, the above-mentioned pronouncements of Judge Vukas and the perspective of Judge Jesus, are pertinent here (see Section 2).

494 South China Sea Arbitration, Award (n 3), para. 515

495 See, Schofield (n 119), 322–340, 333–334.

6.2 *Confirmations and Clarifications in the Definition of Islands*

The South China Sea Tribunal provided a highly detailed, indeed near-forensic, analysis of Article 121 which offers important insights towards clarifying the status of insular features and their capacity to generate maritime entitlements (see Section 3). In particular, the Tribunal's elucidation that the term "rock" is not to be interpreted in a strictly geological sense is a welcome confirmation and accords with the jurisprudence of the ICJ.[496]

Further, the Tribunal's view that the determination of an insular feature's status is based on its natural state prior to human intervention and modification represents a critical step forward in how island status is to be determined. This finding allowed the Tribunal to confirm that reclamation activity cannot transform a feature that is a rock within the meaning of Article 121(3) into a fully entitled island. Reconfirmation was also provided with respect to the status and maritime entitlements of low-tide elevations, artificial islands and submerged features.

The finding that human habitation means more than mere survival such that only features that have a capacity to sustain stable, non-transient community of people to a minimum proper standard provides important guidance on this aspect of Article 121(3). The Tribunal's acknowledgement that such a community need not be large and recognition that a group of features could collectively sustain human habitation or economic life is also a significant development and is illustrative of the Tribunal's concern over the potential impacts of its ruling on small island States (see further below).

With respect to economic life, the link between economic activity and the presence of humans living and that the economic activity should be oriented around the feature itself is logical and was animated by the connection the Tribunal established between Article 121(3) and the consensus at UNCLOS III to codify EEZ entitlements. The finding that economic activity should not be purely extractive or dependant on potential EEZ and continental shelf resources and should involve and benefits the community of the feature also follows this logic and avoids the absurd scenario of a feature escaping the status of an Article 121(3) "rock" solely through the economic activities taking place in the EEZ and continental shelf generated from it. While the Tribunal did not rule out island communities being supported from external support, the requirement that a feature not be disproportionately dependent on outside resources also represents a major development.

496 See, Nicaragua-Colombia case (n 41), para. 37.

The Tribunal did not set objective, yet also arbitrary, numerical tests for these requirements such as minimum number of insular inhabitants, means to assess quality of life or level of economic activity. Nonetheless, it did indicate a number of key factors to be taken into account in the assessment of insular features including the presence of potable fresh water, the presence of vegetation, agricultural potential as well as the presence of fishermen, and commercial operations with a view to determining whether a feature could provide the necessary "food drink and shelter" required for human habitation[497] or to support an economic life for the benefit of the coastal community concerned. This allows for the flexibility necessary to accommodate the immense diversity of island situations and to address the issue of defining island status on a case-by-case basis.

The Tribunal's reliance on historical evidence was both understandable and appropriate in the particular circumstances of the South China Sea where large-scale island building had served to radically change the physical characteristics of many of the insular features under consideration resulting in the natural state of features being obscured or destroyed. However, it can be noted that the historic record is uneven globally and can be limited, for instance in relation to often remote, peripheral insular features. It can also be noted here that the Tribunal appeared to be comfortable with more traditional sources of evidence such as charts and sailing directions as compared with emerging advances in the application of satellite imagery.[498] This suggests that novel proposals to apply new technologies as alternatives to historical evidence, whilst of considerable merit, may not have persuaded this particular Tribunal.[499] However, this has the potential to change in the future as technologies mature, gain wider acceptance and bearing in mind judicial discretion to accept the most convincing evidence in a particular case.

Overall, therefore, the South China Sea Tribunal's systematic and purposeful interpretation of Article 121(3) provides substantial guidance on the definition of island status and therefore represents a highly significant contribution to the law of the sea.

497 South China Sea Arbitration, Award (n 3), para. 490.

498 Such as the multi-spectral analysis of satellite imagery as presented in the present author's report to the Tribunal. See, Schofield et al. (n 79), at 12–16.

499 For example, the proposal that to help inform the determination of the permanence above water of high-tide features analysis could be based on series of high resolution satellite images combined with the latest high resolution tide prediction models and reconstruction of sea level variations based on satellite altimetry. See, Lyons et al. (n 73), at 137.

6.3 *Remaining Uncertainties and Fresh Scope for Conflicting Interpretation*

As noted above, the Tribunal's interpretation of Article 121(3) has undoubtedly provided substantial clarification of the regime of islands. However, there are remaining uncertainties such as with respect high and low tide levels as no preferred vertical datum was indicated, meaning that challenges in identifying low-elevation above high-water features and LTES as well as between LTES and fully submerged features are likely to persist. Moreover, the Tribunal's Award has also raised some fresh issues of interpretation and potential dispute relating to terminology. This arises from the Tribunal's use of words and phrases that are devoid of qualifying tests. Thus, while interpretation of Article 121 of the LOSC has been made much clearer, nonetheless the definition of island status is not entirely straightforward.

For example, with respect to human habitation the requirement that a "stable community" of people for whom the island in question "constitutes a home" is silent regarding how many people this might involve and over what time period.[500] Here, it is of interest that in 1993 Van Dyke and Bennett presciently suggested limiting extended maritime zones to those insular formations "capable of sustaining a resident or a nearby stable community of persons." They went on to advocate a "commonsense approach" to interpreting what the term "stable community" whereby "[c]learly, five persons would be too few to constitute a stable community, but 50 very well could serve as a population of sufficient size."[501] Of course this is only one suggestion from the literature but one from an eminent law of the sea scholar in Jon Van Dyke and it therefore represents a potentially helpful marker. That said, the number of people involved in forming a community of people will surely vary according to a particular island's unique situation, influenced by location and climate as well as socio-cultural factors.

The qualitative elements to human habitation, particularly the meaning or level of a "proper" standard of living, are also unclear as this seems to be a malleable phrase with potentially huge socio-economic and cultural variability in its application. Further, the degree of allowable external support before habitation or economic life on a feature becomes overly dependent on outside resources remains to be determined, once again on a case-by-case basis.[502] Moreover, the degree to which several islands can be linked or form a "constellation" so as to collectively support human habitation or an economic life will require further exploration (see below).

500 Ibid., paras 497 and 535.

501 Van Dyke and Bennett (n 255), at 79.

502 South China Sea Arbitration, Award (n 3), para. 550.

The role of emerging technology influencing the changing way that humans live and work may also impact on the assessment of human habitability and economic life and how this may well evolve and change in the future. Evidentiary challenges may well also arise with respect to assessing the natural condition of features prior to human intervention.[503]

Thus, the Tribunal's Award introduces new terminology without abstract definitions. Such fresh and themselves potentially ambiguous terms will no doubt be subject to future debates among law of the sea scholars and practitioners, as with the interpretational leeway built into the Award, clearly with the interests of small island States in mind.

6.4 *Scope for Flexibility*

It follows from the above that the Tribunal's Award offers interpretational leeway, particularly for small island States, in its conclusions on Article 121(3). With regard to "human habitation" the Tribunal's finding, without determining a precise number, was that the community involved "need not necessarily be large" and that, for example, "in remote atolls a few individuals or family groups could well suffice"[504] is significant. Moreover, periodic rather than permanent habitation by nomadic people "could also constitute habitation."[505] The Tribunal noted that the record of discussions at UNCLOS III revealed "a great deal of sensitivity to the livelihoods of the populations of small island nations."[506]

Thus, where a fully entitled feature "will ordinarily only possess an economic life of its own if it is also inhabited by a stable community of people", an exception to this scenario is, according to the Tribunal, where populations are sustaining themselves through a "network" or "constellation" of related maritime features.[507] The Tribunal reached this view on the basis that it was "conscious that remote island populations often make use of a number of islands, sometimes spread over significant distances, for sustenance and livelihoods."[508] It can therefore be anticipated, that such States will seek to deploy arguments based on the historical use of groups of islands to support

503 Ibid., para. 511.

504 Ibid., para. 542.

505 Ibid.

506 Ibid. The Tribunal further observed that while an indigenous population of a feature "would obviously suffice" to fulfil the human habitation criterion, a non-indigenous population could also do so "if the intent of the population was truly to reside in and make their lives on the islands in question."

507 Ibid., para. 544.

508 Ibid., para. 547.

human habitation and economic activity.[509] No objective criteria were provided as to how many features might comprise such a network or constellation of islands, how close together or in other ways connected or related to one another these features need to.

While this clearly provides useful scope for interpretive leeway, the counterpoint is that there is also scope for future dispute on this point. While the Tribunal has been appropriately mindful of the needs of small island developing States, the application to other geographical and climatic contexts, such as with respect to high latitude islands, remains to be seen. However, the Tribunal's emphasis on assessment of insular features on a "case-by-case basis",[510] and with "due regard" to the possibility that a group of islands may collectively provide for human habitation or economic life allows for the particular circumstances of island groups and their communities to be taken into consideration.[511]

6.5 *Charting a New Course towards Defining Islands: A Three-stage Process*

Through its detailed analysis of Article 121 of the LOSC the Tribunal has charted a fresh approach to the determination of island status under the international law of the sea. Arguably this amounts to a three-stage process, unconsciously or otherwise echoing that for the delimitation of maritime boundaries.[512]

At the first stage it needs to be ascertained that a features, in its natural state, fulfils the requirements of Article 121(1). That is, whether an insular feature is a naturally formed feature that is composed of land, is surrounded by water and is above water at high-tide. Previous ICJ jurisprudence has determined that it is immaterial how large features are and what they are composed of so long as they are naturally formed.[513] The requirement that a feature is surrounded by water is seemingly straightforward. Accordingly, potential for dispute will tend to relate to confirmation that a given feature is above high water level, in contrast to one that is covered at high-tide but uncovered at low tide or one that is permanently below low water level. This determination results in the

509 It is notable here that the Award refers to a contribution of the Micronesian delegate to UNCLOS III, indicating that the Tribunal had the interests of small island developing States in mind (ibid., para. 497).

510 Ibid., para. 546.

511 Ibid., paras 497 and 546.

512 Black Sea case (n 122), para. 116. See also, SB Kaye, 'Assessing the Impact of the South China Sea Arbitration on Small Island States: A Case Study of Kiribati' (2019) 34(4) *International Journal of Marine and Coastal Law* 778–799.

513 See, Nicaragua-Colombia case (41), paras 35–37.

feature in question being respectively subject to LOSC Article 121, Article 13, or simply a component part of the sea floor (be it part of a coastal State's territorial sea, continental shelf or part of the Area). Nevertheless, this is something that can be determined with the aid of contemporary observations, including ever improving technologies such as satellite derived bathymetry, coupled with historical observations as demonstrated by the South China Sea case (see Sections 2 and 3).

At the second stage evidence of the "objective physical conditions" of a particular feature will "ordinarily suffice" to categorise an above high-tide feature into a fully entitled island or a "rock" within the meaning of Article 121(2) and (3) of the LOSC, respectively.[514] The Tribunal commented that:

> If a feature is entirely barren of vegetation and lacks drinkable water and the foodstuffs necessary even for basic survival, it will be apparent that it also lacks the capacity to sustain human habitation. The opposite conclusion could likewise be reached where the physical characteristics of a large feature make it definitively habitable.[515]

The third stage involves the examination of borderline cases as discussed above, with the Tribunal pointing to the assessment of a series of key indicators for human habitation or economic life including the presence of potable water, vegetation, agriculture, fishing activities and other commercial operations to determine island status.[516] In the context of features "close to the line", physical conditions alone were considered to be insufficient.[517] Under such circumstances, the Tribunal viewed the "most reliable" evidence relating to the capacity of a feature to be the historical record of the use to which it had been put.[518] This step-by-step procedure to analyse insular features and determine their status also represents an important development in the definition of islands.

6.6 *Implications*

Although the Tribunal's Award was specifically focussed on insular features in the South China Sea, and its findings are clearly only binding on China and the

514 South China Sea Arbitration, Award (n 3), para. 548.

515 Ibid.

516 See also Gullett (n 126), at 23–24.

517 South China Sea Arbitration, Award (n 3), para. 548.

518 Ibid., para. 549. Here it can be noted that the Tribunal allowed for exceptional circumstances such as "[w]ar, pollution and environmental harm" that may have prevented an otherwise inhabitable island from being inhabited for a prolonged period.

Philippines in its specifics, the Tribunal's Award nonetheless has great potential relevance to insular features elsewhere as well as broader implications both within and beyond the South China Sea.

6.6.1 Implications of the Arbitration Award for the South China Sea disputes

In accordance with the LOSC, and given declaration by China under Article 298, the Arbitration Tribunal in the Philippines v. China case could only address issues arising from the interpretation and application of the Convention.[519] This factor, coupled with the fact that the case directly involved only the Philippines and China among the South China Sea claimants (despite the latter opting for not taking part in the proceedings), meant that the Tribunal could not resolve the core sovereignty issues at stake – that is, determining which State has sovereignty over which disputed islands in the South China Sea. Nonetheless, the Award of the Tribunal has potentially major implications for the South China Sea disputes, both legally and geographically.

The legal basis for any claims on the part of China to historic rights to the waters within the Nine-Dash line was essentially dismissed by the Tribunal.[520] This ruling, coupled with the Tribunal's finding that none of the Spratly Islands or Scarborough Reef is capable of generating extended maritime claims has the potential to radically reshape the South China Sea disputes. This is because the Tribunal's ruling provides substantial legal clarification with direct implications for the extent of claims to maritime jurisdiction in the South China Sea and thus the extent of areas of disputed waters. Indeed, the spatial implications of the Tribunal's ruling are striking: from encompassing around 80 per cent of the South China Sea (see Figure 9), the extent of disputed waters would be dramatically reduced to 12 M pockets of contested territorial sea surrounding islands, sovereignty over which is disputed (see Figure 10). Additionally, overlapping maritime claims and disputes would remain between adjacent neighbouring South China Sea coastal States (see below and Figures 7 and 10). The Tribunal's Award, if implemented, therefore clarifies and dramatically reduces areas of overlapping maritime claims and thereby arguably assists in the resolution of the South China Sea disputes.

519 See, Section III(A) above.

520 Ibid., para. 1203(B)(2). See also, for example, R Beckman, '"Deliberate Ambiguity" and the Demise of China's Claim to Historic Rights in the South China Sea (2016) 1(2) *Asia-Pacific Journal of Ocean Law and Policy* 164–182, at 182.

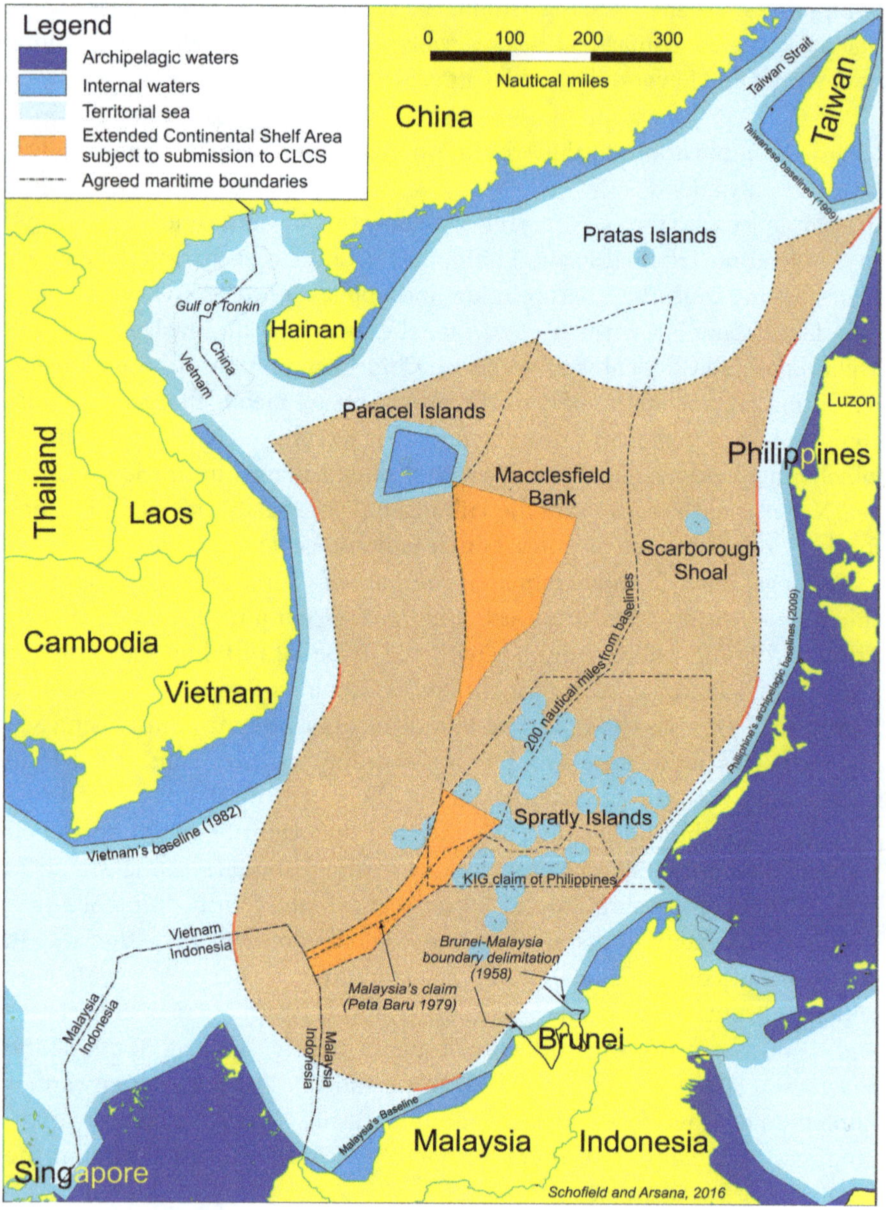

FIGURE 9 Disputed Waters in the South China Sea before the Arbitration Award
SOURCE: PREPARED FOR THE AUTHOR BY I MADE ANDI ARSANA[521]

521 See also, CH Schofield, 'Contested ocean spaces: A case study of the South China Sea', *Geography Review* (November 2017) 31(2) 22–26, at 26; and CH Schofield, 'Conflicting Maritime Visions of the South China Sea', *ASEAN Focus* (June 2020) 33(2) 15–17, at 16.

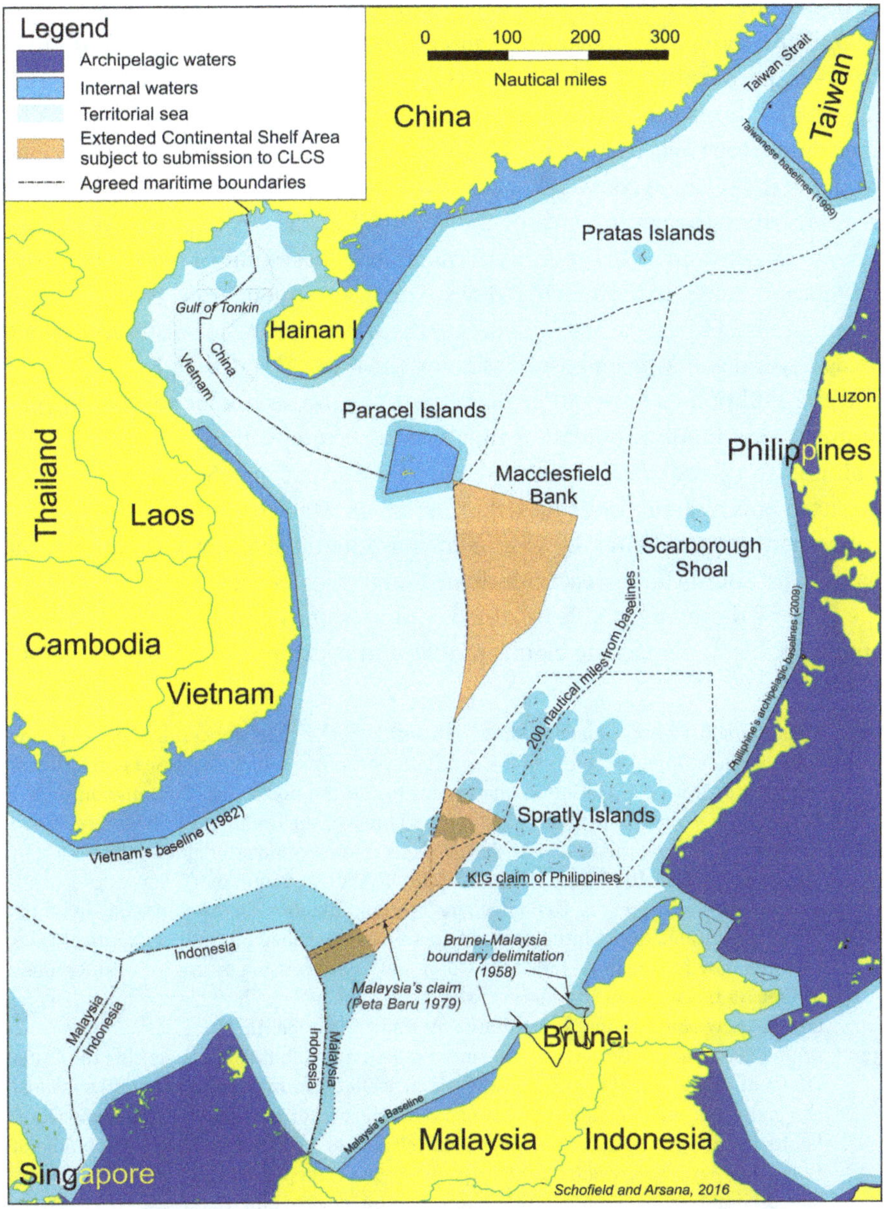

FIGURE 10 Disputed Waters in the South China Sea after the Implementation of the Arbitration Award
SOURCE: PREPARED FOR THE AUTHOR BY I MADE ANDI ARSANA[522]

522 Ibid., at 25.

In keeping with the Award, the Philippines and, by extension, Malaysia, Brunei and Indonesia, are free to claim rights over the sea to 200 M from their coasts as part of their exclusive economic zones (EEZs). Additionally, the ruling also confirms the existence of a pocket of high seas in the central part of the South China Sea, beyond the limits of EEZ claims from surrounding mainland and main island coasts.

Concerning the central area of the South China Sea or high seas pocket, it was already clear prior to the Arbitral case that at least some of the South China Sea coastal States had opposing views. This was evident from the May 2009 submissions of Malaysia and Vietnam to the CLCS relating to continental shelf areas beyond 200 M from baselines along the coast.[523] Further, Brunei, China and the Philippines have either made partial submissions or submitted preliminary information indicating that they also intend to make submissions claiming an extended continental shelf in the South China Sea.[524]

These submissions indicated that as far as Malaysia and Vietnam were concerned areas of 'outer' or 'extended' continental shelf exist in the central part of the South China Sea, underlying a high seas pocket, indicating that in the view of these States at least, the disputed islands of the South China Sea are incapable of generating claims to EEZ and continental shelf rights. China

523 Malaysia and Vietnam made a joint submission to the CLCS concerning an area lying between their opposite coasts in the southern part of the South China Sea and Vietnam a further submission relating to an area further to the north. See, Commission on the Limits of the Continental Shelf (CLCS) Outer Limits of the Continental Shelf beyond 200 Nautical Miles from the Baselines: Submissions to the Commission: Joint Submission by Malaysia and Socialist Republic of Viet Nam, Executive Summary (6 May 2009), available at http://www.un.org/Depts/los/clcs_new/submissions_files/submission_mysvnm_33_2009.htm; and, CLCS Outer Limits of the Continental Shelf beyond 200 Nautical Miles from the Baselines: Submission to the Commission: Submission by the Socialist Republic of Viet Nam, Executive Summary (7 May 2009), available at http://www.un.org/Depts/los/clcs_new/submissions_files/submission_vnm_37_2009.htm.

524 Brunei-Darussalam, 'Brunei-Darussalam's Preliminary Submission concerning the Outer Limits of its Continental Shelf', 12 May 2009, available at http://www.un.org/Depts/los/clcs_new/commission_preliminary.htm; Preliminary Information Indicative of the Outer Limits of the Continental Shelf Beyond 200 Nautical Miles of the People's Republic of China, 11 May 2009, available at http://www.un.org/depts/los/clcs_new/submissions_files/preliminary/chn2009preliminaryinformation_english.pdf; CLCS Outer Limits of the Continental Shelf beyond 200 Nautical Miles from the Baselines: Submissions to the Commission: Submission by the Republic of the Philippines, 19 July 2012, available at http://www.un.org/Depts/los/clcs_new/submissions_files/submission_phl_22_2009.htm; CLCS Outer Limits of the Continental Shelf beyond 200 Nautical Miles from the Baselines: Submissions to the Commission: Submission by the People's Republic of China, 14 December 2012, available at http://www.un.org/Depts/los/clcs_new/submissions_files/submission_chn_63_2012.htm; accessed 6 April 2014.

objected to these submissions stating that not only did it have sovereignty over the disputed islands in the South China Sea but using language suggesting that it was claiming territorial sea areas around the disputed islands (sovereignty over "adjacent waters") and EEZ and continental shelf rights around them ("sovereign rights and jurisdiction over the relevant waters as well as the seabed and subsoil thereof").[525]

What has also become increasingly clear subsequent to the Tribunal's ruling is that South China Sea coastal States other than China are increasingly relying on its Award in their approach to maritime claims in the South China Sea.[526] This was made clear through the diplomatic correspondence of both littoral and extra-regional States arising from a further submission relating to continental shelf rights in the central part of the South China Sea on the part of Malaysia of 12 December 2019.[527] China protested through a note verbale directed to the Secretary-General of the United Nations that it had sovereignty over the Spratly Islands (Nansha Quandao) and Scarborough Reef (Huangyang Dao) and their "adjacent waters", sovereign rights and jurisdiction over the "relevant waters as well as the seabed and subsoil thereof" – language that can be taken to correspond to territorial sea and EEZ/continental shelf rights respectively – as well as "historic rights in the South China Sea". China further asserted that its sovereignty and jurisdictional claims in the South China Sea were supported by "abundant historical and legal evidence".[528]

In their counter-protests, both Indonesia and the Philippines made direct reference to the Arbitral Tribunal's Award in their diplomatic notes, with respect to its decision that none of the Spratly Islands generate EEZ or continental shelf entitlements, while the language contained in Vietnam's diplomatic note is entirely consistent with its findings.[529] As Beckman has noted,

525 Communications Received with regard to the Joint Submission made by Malaysia and Vietnam to the CLCS (n 523), China (7 May 2009 and 14 April 2011).

526 It therefore appears that Oxman's prediction that the Award will "unquestionably" impact the perceptions of both States that "border and use the South China Sea" has been proved correct. See, Oxman (n 423), at 19.

527 Malaysia Partial Submission, Executive Summary (12 December 2019), available at https://www.un.org/Depts/los/clcs_new/submissions_files/mys85_2019/20171128_MYS_ES_DOC_001_secured.pdf.

528 Communication Received with regards to the submission made by Malaysia (ibid.), China (23 March 2020), available at https://www.un.org/Depts/los/clcs_new/submissions_files/submission_mys_12_12_2019.html.

529 Communications Received with regards to the submission made by Malaysia (ibid.), Indonesia (26 May), the Philippines (6 March, communication 2) and Vietnam (30 March and 10 April), available at https://www.un.org/Depts/los/clcs_new/submissions_files/submission_mys_12_12_2019.html.

these diplomatic communications are publically available and distributed to all UN members and therefore provide a strong confirmation that these States both reaffirm their reliance on the LOSC to govern maritime entitlements and "in effect consider the Arbitral Award as an authoritative interpretation of the law" concerning maritime claims in the South China Sea.[530]

The Arbitral Award therefore appears to have transformed the South China Sea maritime disputes geographically, in terms of the spatial extent of overlapping maritime claims, and legally.[531] The key caveat here, though, is that this only holds true should the Award be implemented. China has, however, consistently and vociferously rejected the ruling and there are no legal mechanisms by which it can be enforced. China is therefore likely to maintain not only its claims to sovereignty over all of the disputed South China Sea islands but to maritime areas within the nine-dashed line as well. Despite this, commentators such as Kraska have argued that "the normative force and authority of the Award decision and UNCLOS will grow."[532]

This scenario of opposing perceptions or visions of maritime entitlements in the South China, Sea competing maritime claims backed up by enforcement activities not only compromises the protection of the region's precious marine biodiversity and management of its abundant fisheries resources[533] but sets the scene for future conflict as China seeks to assert what it views as its historic rights in the South China Sea while other coastal States attempt to access the resources, notably fisheries resources and hydrocarbons deposits, that lie within what they firmly regard as 'their' waters proximate to their mainland and main island coasts.[534] This represents an ominous potential threat to regional stability and freedom of navigation through waterways of global significance.[535]

530 R Beckman, 'US joins "lawfare" by diplomatic notes over Chinese claims in the S. China Sea', The Straits Times, 10 June 2020, available https://www.straitstimes.com/opinion/us-joins-lawfare-by-diplomatic-notes-over-chinese-claims-in-s-china-sea.

531 Davenport (n 423), at 85–86.

532 Kraska (n 399), at 58.

533 See R Sumalia and W Cheung, *Boom or Bust: The Future of Fishing in the South China Sea* (ADM Capital Foundation, Hong Kong, 2015), available from http://www.admcf.org/wordpress/wp-content/uploads/2015/11/FishSCSea03_11-FINAL-FINAL.pdf.

534 See, ibid.; and, J Kraska, 'China's Maritime Militia Upends Rules on Naval Warfare', *The Diplomat*, 10 August 2015, available from http://thediplomat.com/2015/08/chinas-maritime-militia-upends-rules-on-naval-warfare/.

535 For example, it has been estimated that US$3.4 trillion in trade passed through the South China Sea in 2016, including over 64 per cent of China's maritime trade. See, Center for Strategic and International Studies (CSIS) China Power, 'How much trade

While there appeared to be a desire on the part of China to de-escalate regional tensions in the immediate aftermath of the Tribunal handing down its Award, is seems clear that the Award has led to a hardening in China's claims.[536] Indeed, in 2020 China was involved in a series of coercive measures suggesting that it is likely to continue to pressure other South China Sea coastal States, especially over marine resource issues. This is evidenced by fisheries-related confrontations between China and Indonesia off the Natuna Islands.[537] Additionally, China has either undertaken oil and gas exploration activities of its own or sought to impede those of other South China Sea coastal States in waters proximate to Brunei Darussalam and Malaysia,[538] as well as Vietnam.[539]

China has also undertaken fresh acts of administration designed to support its claims in the South China Sea. For example, in April 2020 China unilaterally named 80 geographical features, including 55 submerged ones, in the South China Sea, apparently in order to assert its "sovereignty and sovereign rights".[540] Additionally, the city of Sansha, located on China's Hainan Island, has established two new districts to "administer waters in the South China Sea"

---

transits the South China Sea?', 2 August 2017, available at https://chinapower.csis.org/much-trade-transits-south-china-sea/.

536 See, for example, Zhang (n 420), at 447–454.

537 See, for example, 'Indonesia rejects China's claims over South China Sea', *Channel New Asia*, 1 January 2020, available at https://www.channelnewsasia.com/news/asia/indonesia-jakarta-rejects-claims-south-china-sea-natuna-islands-12225464; K Siregar, 'Indonesia deploys 4 additional warships to Natuna amid standoff with Chinese warships', *Channel News Asia*, 6 January 2020, available at, https://www.channelnewsasia.com/news/asia/indonesia-china-natuna-islands-dispute-south-china-sea-12237456?cid=h3_referral_inarticlelinks_24082018_cna; D Grossman, 'Why is China Pressing Indonesia Again Over Its Maritime Claims', *World Politics Review*, 16 January 2020, available at, https://www.worldpoliticsreview.com/articles/28476/why-is-china-pressing-indonesia-again-over-the-natuna-islands.

538 See, 'The South China Sea: Chinese ship Haiyang Dizhi 8 seen near Malaysian waters, security sources say', *South China Morning Post*, 18 April 2020, available at https://www.scmp.com/news/asia/southeast-asia/article/3080510/south-china-sea-chinese-ship-haiyang-dizhi-8-seen-near; and, '5-nation face-off in high-seas energy tussle off Malaysia', *The Straits Times*, 25 April 2020, available at https://www.straitstimes.com/asia/se-asia/5-nation-face-off-in-high-seas-energy-tussle-off-malaysia.

539 See, for example, 'Chinese Survey Vessel Returns to Disputed Vietnamese Waters', *The Maritime Executive*, 15 April 2020, available at https://www.maritime-executive.com/article/chinese-survey-vessel-returns-to-disputed-vietnamese-waters.

540 See, K Huang, 'Beijing marks out claims in South China Sea by naming geographical features', *South China Morning Post*, 20 April 2020, available at https://www.scmp.com/news/china/diplomacy/article/3080721/beijing-marks-out-claims-south-china-sea-naming-geographical.

including the Xisha and Zhongsha Islands.[541] While the Xisha Islands correspond in English to the Paracel Islands, as mentioned above, the Zhongsha "Islands" comprise the entirely and permanently submerged Macclesfield Bank[542] and the 5–7 "miniscule" coral protrusions that are the only above high-tide features present on Scarborough Reef.[543]

The Award also has implications for the delimitation of maritime boundaries in the South China Sea. The Tribunal drew a distinction between consideration of the existence of entitlement to maritime zones and a dispute over the delimitation of such zones where they overlap.[544] Nonetheless, the Tribunal's determination that all of the Spratly Islands as well as Scarborough Reef are rocks necessarily has significant implications for the scope of maritime entitlements involving these features. This, in turn, impacts on the extent to which such entitlements overlap and therefore the existence of potential maritime boundaries to delimit.

On the basis of the Award potential territorial sea boundary situations exist between those features found to be naturally formed and above high-tide rocks of the Spratly Islands group but this fundamentally depends on the resolution of the sovereignty disputes over these features. Additionally, potential lateral maritime boundaries exist between, the coastal States bordering the South China Sea.[545]

In addition to being deployed to support the maritime claims of South China Sea coastal States other than China/Taiwan, it is also increasingly evident that the Tribunal's Award provides the basis for the positions of extra-regional but interested States, such as Australia and the United States, on maritime claims related to islands in the South China Sea. Concerning islands issues the US communication of 1 June 2020 arising from the above-mentioned CLCS submission of Malaysia and China's responses to it states that:

541 See, L Xin, 'Sansha city establishes two districts for better management', *Global Times*, 18 April 2020, available at, https://www.globaltimes.cn/content/1186004.shtml.

542 See, UKHO (n 389).

543 South China Sea Arbitration, Award (n 3), paras 555–556.

544 South China Sea Arbitration, Award on Jurisdiction (n 3), para 154.

545 Clockwise from the northwest, China and Vietnam, China/Taiwan and the Philippines, the Philippines and Malaysia, Malaysia and Brunei, Malaysia and Indonesia, and Indonesia and Vietnam. See, CH Schofield, 'An Incomplete Maritime Map: Progress and Challenges in the Delimitation of Maritime Boundaries in South East Asia', in D Rothwell and D Letts (eds), *Law of the Sea in South East Asia: Environmental, Navigational and Security Challenges* (Routledge: London, 2019) 33–62, at 44–48.

> … the United States objects to any claimed maritime entitlements based on features that are not islands within the meaning of article 121(1) of the Convention and thus do not generate maritime zones of their own under international law. China may not assert sovereignty over, or claim maritime zones derived from, entirely submerged features like Macclesfield Bank or James Shoal, or features like Mischief Reef and Second Thomas Shoal, which in their natural state are low-tide elevations. These positions are consistent with the decision of the Tribunal in The South China Sea Arbitration.[546]

Subsequently, the Australian note of 23 July 2020 was robust in stating that the Australian Government:

> … rejects any claims by China that are inconsistent with the 1982 United Nations Convention on the Law of the Sea (UNCLOS), in particular, maritime claims that do not adhere to its rules on baselines, maritime zones and classification of features.[547]

Australia's communication went on to state that:

> Australia also rejects China's claims to maritime zones generated by submerged features, or low tide elevations in a manner inconsistent with UNCLOS. Land building activities or other forms of artificial transformation cannot change the classification of a feature under UNCLOS. There is no legal basis for a maritime feature to generate maritime entitlements beyond those generated under UNCLOS by that feature in its natural state. In this respect, the Australian Government does not accept that artificially transformed features can ever acquire the status of an island under Article 121(1) of UNCLOS.[548]

---

546 Communications Received with regards to the submission made by Malaysia (n 527), United States (1 June), available at https://www.un.org/Depts/los/clcs_new/submissions_files/submission_mys_12_12_2019.html. The US position was underscored by a statement by the Secretary of State Pompeo on 13 July 2020. See also, MR Pompeo, 'U.S. Position on Maritime Claims in the South China Sea', Press Statement, 13 July 2020, available at https://www.state.gov/u-s-position-on-maritime-claims-in-the-south-china-sea/.

547 Communications Received with regards to the submission made by Malaysia (n 527), Australia (23 July), available at https://www.un.org/Depts/los/clcs_new/submissions_files/submission_mys_12_12_2019.html.

548 Ibid. Australia also made reference to Article 60(8) of the LOSC on this point.

Both the Australian and United States notes also rejected China's historic claims in the South China Sea, making direct reference to the findings of the Arbitral Tribunal on these issues, and further rejected any Chinese claims to straight or archipelagic baselines around South China Sea islands.[549] Subsequent Australian and US Ministerial consultations led to a joint statement of 28 July 2020 expressed "serious concerns over recent coercive and destabilizing actions" across the Indo-Pacific region and that "[i]n line with the 2016 decision of the Arbitral Tribunal" the Ministers "affirmed that Beijing's maritime claims are not valid under international law" and that "the 2016 Arbitral Award is final and binding on both parties and emphasized that all claims in the South China Sea must be made and resolved in accordance with international law."[550] Such statements indicate that despite China's non-participation in the arbitration case and rejection of the Tribunal's Award, it nonetheless strongly informs how States within and beyond the South China Sea view maritime claims in the region.

6.6.2 Implications beyond the South China Sea

There seems little doubt that the Tribunal's Award has generally resounded well beyond the South China Sea. For example, Oxman notes that the Award will impact not only on the South China Sea disputes but on "oceans beyond" on the basis of its "authoritative contribution to the law of the sea" and suggests that this may lead to "a tempering of disputes over small features at sea and the entitlements that they generate" and "a decline in gratuitous environmental disruption occasioned by attempts to artificially enhance such features to reinforce claims to maritime jurisdiction."[551] McDorman, has similarly noted that, "[t]he rock or island criteria in the Award may result in States able to more readily reach maritime boundary agreements and adjudicative bodies more readily able to make such determinations".[552]

With respect to State practice, at the time of writing, there was little sign, or indeed likely prospect, of coastal States rolling back their broad maritime claims asserted from small insular features. Indeed, it is notable that even those States that greeted the Award positively and called on China and the Philippines to abide by it have made no move to revise their own maritime

549 See, Communications Received with regards to the submission made by Malaysia (n 527), United States (1 June) and Australia (23 July 2020).

550 United States Department of State, 'Joint Statement on Australia-U.S. Ministerial consultations (AUSMIN) 2020', Media Note, 28 July 2020, available at https://www.state.gov/joint-statement-on-australia-u-s-ministerial-consultations-ausmin-2020/.

551 See, Oxman (423).

552 See, McDorman (n 459).

claims from insular features that would arguably struggle to meet the standard for fully entitled island status set by the Tribunal. This is hardly surprising since such modifications to their claims would entail potentially significant reductions in the scope of their maritime claims and thus rights over the valuable marine resources within those claimed areas. This suggests that coastal States are likely to be highly resistant to change and are likely to emphasise the fact that the Award is binding solely on its parties, China and the Philippines and, further, that the Tribunal itself noted that evaluation of particular islands should be conducted on a case-by-case basis.[553]

While 'roll backs' to claims to a 200 M zone on the basis of reclassifying a feature as a rock within the meaning of Article 121(3) analogous to that of the UK for the isolated rocky pinnacle of Rockall appear unlikely,[554] there are some indications that States will seek to deploy the Award's findings, albeit where they work in their favour. For example, in 2017 Indonesia revised its official map, seemingly on the basis of the Tribunal's Award regarding the status of features in the South China Sea,[555] to show a more advanced unilateral 'forward position' with respect to neighbouring States where a maritime boundary has yet to be delimited. In particular, Palau's southernmost islands are depicted on Indonesia's map as being fully enclaved in pockets of territorial sea while the southernmost islands of Palau's main group of islands, located further north, are shown as being semi-enclaved and only accorded 12 M territorial seas in the direction of Indonesia.[556]

This illustrates how the Award also has implications for future maritime boundary delimitation negotiations involving islands. It can also be anticipated that States will invoke the Tribunal's findings in the context of international litigation cases involving islands, where key basepoints for one side are located on insular features where the capacity to support habitation or degree of economic life can be challenged against the high threshold set by the South China Sea Tribunal's Award.

553 South China Sea Arbitration, Award (n 3), para. 546.

554 See, MacDonald (n 109), at 627–628.

555 See, Badan Informasi Geospasial [Agency for Geospatial Information] (BIG), *Peta Negara Kesatuan Republik Indonesia* [Map of the Unitary State of the Republic of Indonesia], (Cibinong, 2017).

556 Ibid. It can, however, be noted that Palau could counter any such claim based on the South China Sea Award not only on the basis that it is only binding on China and the Philippines but also by taking advantage of the scope for flexibility seemingly aimed at small island States built into the Award.

6.7 *The Last Word on the Issue?*

As the first detailed international judicial interpretation of Article 121 and, hence, Part VIII of the LOSC, on the "Regime of islands", the South China Sea Tribunal's unanimous Award represents an important step in the clarification of the international law of the sea. Overall, the Tribunal has done much to clarify the challenging issue of the definition of islands. The necessary scope for flexibility embedded in the Award does, however, also provide significant latitude for differing interpretations over terminology and thresholds lacking objective criteria.

Is the South China Sea Tribunal's Award the last word on the question of the interpretation of Article 121? Almost certainly not, as the law of the sea continues to evolve over time. As yes, the Award has had scant impact on expansive State practice. Here, it appears that many coastal States are waiting and watching, not only to see whether other States are amending their practice but whether the Award in the South China Sea case will be echoed and underpinned by future jurisprudence. As several commentators have noted, this remains to be seen, with certain commentators suggesting that it is uncertain whether another international judicial body may reach a narrow a view of the application of rocks within the meaning of Article 121(3) of LOSC and thus an outcome that is more palatable to certain coastal States may be forthcoming (see Section 5).

Certainly it is perfectly possible that future case law may yet further elucidate our understanding of the definition of islands in international law. However, it can also be observed that international courts and arbitral tribunals, while clearly capable of changing their views and approaches over time, have tended to be respectful of previous rulings with their decisions invariably laced with references back to aspects of earlier judgments.[557] Thus, while international judicial decisions are undoubtedly only binding on the parties to the particular case and each case features its own particular facts and circumstances, nonetheless, the international judicial and arbitral decisions, such as the Tribunal's Award, tend to be influential. Indeed, according to one eminent commentator, writing in relation to maritime boundary delimitation cases in particular, the rulings of such international courts and tribunals "carry special weight" largely

557 Especially so with respect to ICJ rulings which have been frequently cited in the awards of arbitral tribunals and the ITLOS. Conversely, it is rare for the ICJ to cite the decisions of arbitral tribunals.

because of the "relative scarcity of authoritative pronouncements."[558] This would clearly appear to apply with respect to the South China Sea Tribunal's Award which, as noted above, is the sole detailed international judicial interpretation of the regime of islands.

Changes to the definition of islands may well occur against the backdrop of a deepening climate crisis. There is now negligible doubt in the scientific community that the global ocean is warming, acidifying and becoming increasingly deoxygenated. This has profound implications for future insular status as a consequence, in particular, of sea level rise as well as the increased frequency and intensity of extreme weather events.[559] This raises the dire prospect of island becoming more and more uninhabitable over time and, ultimately, islands disappearing altogether.

While such radically changing circumstances or a future case could indeed lead to an alternative interpretation, the South China Sea Award is, for the moment at least, the sole detailed international judicial analysis of the regime of islands and as such it stands as the authoritative interpretation which should be welcomed by those favouring a clearer understanding of these problematic provisions of the LOSC as well as those who advocate the progressive development of and the international law of the sea more generally.

558 JI Charney, 'Progress in International Maritime Boundary Delimitation Law' (1994) 88 *American Journal of International Law* 227–256, at 227.

559 With respect to sea rise specifically, the IPCC has asserted, with very high confidence, that the acceleration in global mean sea level rise detected in recent decades has been due to "increasing rates of loss from the Greenland and Antarctic ice sheets" together with continued glacier ice mass loss and ocean thermal expansion. See, for example, IPCC (n 98).

List of Figures

Acknowledgments

The author wishes to acknowledge the generous financial support provided by The Nippon Foundation of Japan. The author also acknowledges research support through the Australian Research Council Discovery Grant DP180101996, held jointly with colleagues Professor Stuart Kaye of the Australian National Centre for Ocean Resources and Security (ANCORS) and Professor Michael Petterson, Auckland University of Technology.

The author is indebted to Dr I Made Andi Arsana of the Department of Geodetic and Geomatic Engineering at Universitas Gadjah Mada, Indonesia for his kind assistance in preparing the figures included in this study.

Figures 1, 4 and 8 were produced by Dr Arsana and the present author for inclusion in the International Hydrographic Organization (IHO) and International Association of Geodesy (IAG) *Manual on Technical Aspects of the United Nations Convention on the Law of the Sea* – 1982 (TALOS Manual). These figures are reproduced with the kind permission of the IHO and IAG subject to the following notice:

Material from IHO-IAG publication C-51, *A Manual on Technical Aspects of the United Nations Convention on the Law of the Sea* – 1982 (TALOS), Edition 5.0.0 dated June 2014 is reproduced with the permission of Professor Clive Schofield and Dr I Made Andi Arsana, authors of the animated graphics, and of the Secretariat of the International Hydrographic Organization (IHO) and the Executive Council of the International Association of Geodesy (IAG) (Permission N° 8/2020) acting for the International Hydrographic Organization (IHO) and the International Association of Geodesy (IAG), which do not accept responsibility for the correctness of the material as reproduced: in case of doubt, the IHO-IAG's authentic text shall prevail. The incorporation of material sourced from IHO-IAG shall not be construed as constituting an endorsement by IHO or IAG of this product.

The author is also indebted to the Institute for Southeast Asian Studies (ISEAS) for permission to reproduce Figure 3; Professor Martin Pratt and Ms Elizabeth Buxton of the International Boundaries Research Unit (now IBRU: Centre for Borders Research) for permission to reproduce Figure 5; and to Professor David Freestone, editor of the *International Journal of Marine and Coastal Law* and Ms Marie Sheldon, Publishing Director, International Law, Brill/Nijhoff for permission to reproduce Figures 6 and 7.

Author Biography

Clive Schofield
is Professor and Head of Research at the WMU-Sasakawa Global Ocean Institute, World Maritime University (WMU) in Malmö, Sweden. He began his academic career with the International Boundaries Research Unit (IBRU) at the University of Durham, UK and since 2004 has been associated with the Australian National Centre for Ocean Resources and Security (ANCORS), University of Wollongong (UOW), Australia. He is a Distinguished Fellow of the Law of the Sea Institute (LOSI) at the Law School of the University of California, Berkeley, is a Global Associate of the Centre for International Law (CIL) at the National University of Singapore and teaches on the Law of the Sea programme at Harvard Law School. He holds a PhD (Geography) from the University of Durham, UK, and an LLM from the University of British Columbia, Canada.

Clive's research interests relate to international boundaries and particularly maritime boundary delimitation, marine jurisdictional issues and geo-technical issues in the law of the sea on which he has published over 200 scholarly publications. He is an International Hydrographic Office (IHO)-nominated Observer on the Advisory Board on the Law of the Sea (ABLOS) and is a member of the International Law Association's Committee on International Law and Sea Level Rise. He has also been actively involved in the peaceful settlement of boundary and territory disputes by providing advice to governments engaged in boundary negotiations and in dispute settlement cases before international courts and tribunals, including serving as an independent expert witness in the international arbitration case between the Philippines and China.

References

American Society of International Law (ASIL), 'The Regime of Islands in the Aftermath of the South China Sea Arbitration', ASIL 2017 Conference panel, *Proceedings of the Annual ASIL Meeting* 112 (Cambridge University Press: Cambridge, 2018).

Anderson, DH, 'British Accession to the UN Convention on the Law of the Sea' (1997) 46 *International and Comparative Law Quarterly* 761–786.

Anderson, DH, 'Some Aspects of the Regime of Islands and the Law of the Sea' 32 (2017) *International Journal of Marine and Coastal Law* 316–331.

Anderson, DH, *The importance of the tidal datum in the definition of maritime limits and boundaries*, Maritime Briefing, 2(7) (International Boundaries Research Unit: Durham 2000).

Asia Maritime Transparency Initiative (AMTI) 'Occupation and Island Building' available at https://amti.csis.org/island-tracker/.

AMTI, 'Malaysia Island Tracker', available at https://amti.csis.org/island-tracker/malaysia/.

AMTI, 'Philippines Island Tracker', available at https://amti.csis.org/island-tracker/philippines/.

AMTI, 'Vietnam Island Tracker', available at https://amti.csis.org/island-tracker/vietnam/.

AMTI, 'China Island Tracker', available at https://amti.csis.org/island-tracker/china/.

AMTI, 'Arbitration support tracker', available at https://amti.csis.org/arbitration-support-tracker/.

Australian Antarctic Division, "About Heard Island", available at http://www.heardisland.aq/about/location_geography.html.

Australian Government, "The Australian Continent", available from https://www.australia.gov.au/about-australia/our-country/the-australian-continent.

Badan Informasi Geospasial [Agency for Geospatial Information] (BIG), *Peta Negara Kesatuan Republik Indonesia* [Map of the Unitary State of the Republic of Indonesia], (BIG, Cibinong, 2017).

Beazley, PB, 'Half-Effect Applied to Equidistance Lines' (1979) 56 *International Hydrographic Review* 153–160.

Beazley, PB, *Maritime limits and baselines: a guide to their delineation*, Special Publication No.2 (3rd ed., The Hydrographic Society, 1987).

Beazley, P, *Technical Aspects of Maritime Boundary Delimitation, Maritime Briefing*, 1(2), (International Boundaries Research Unit: Durham, 1994).

Beckman, R, '"Deliberate Ambiguity" and the Demise of China's Claim to Historic Rights in the South China Sea' (2016) 1 *Asia-Pacific Journal of Ocean Law and Policy* 164–182.

Beckman, R and CH Schofield, 'Defining EEZ Claims from Islands: A Potential South China Sea Change', (2014) 29(2) *The International Journal of Marine and Coastal Law* 193–243.

Beckman, R, 'US joins "lawfare" by diplomatic notes over Chinese claims in the S. China Sea', The Straits Times, 10 June 2020, available https://www.straitstimes.com/opinion/us-joins-lawfare-by-diplomatic-notes-over-chinese-claims-in-s-china-sea.

Beckman, R and CH Schofield, 'Moving Beyond Disputes over Island Sovereignty: ICJ Decision Sets Stage for Maritime Boundary Delimitation in the Singapore Strait' (2009) 40, *Ocean Development and International Law* 1–35.

Birnie, P, A Boyle and C Redgwell, *International Law and the Environment*, 3rd edition (Oxford University Press: Oxford, 2009).

Brown, F.D, 'Rockall and the Limits of national jurisdiction of the UK' (1978) 2 *Marine Policy* 181–211.

Brown, J, A Colling, D Park, J Phillips, D Rothery and J Wright, *Case Studies in Oceanography and Marine Affairs* (Oxford, Pergamon Press, 1991).

Carleton, CM and CH Schofield, *Developments in the Technical Determination of Maritime Space: Charts, Datums, Baselines, Maritime Zones and Limits*, Maritime Briefing, 3(3) (International Boundaries Research Unit, Durham, 2001).

Centre for International Law (CIL), 'NUS Satellite Research Project on Insular Geographic Features in the South China Sea', available at, https://cil.nus.edu.sg/south-china-sea-satellite-mapping-project/.

Center for Strategic and International Studies (CSIS) China Power, 'How much trade transits the South China Sea?', 2 August 2017, available at https://chinapower.csis.org/much-trade-transits-south-china-sea/.

Charney, JI, 'Progress in International Maritime Boundary Delimitation Law' (1994) 88(2) *American Journal of International Law* 227–256.

Charney, JI, 'Rocks that cannot sustain human habitation' (1999) 93(4) *American Journal of International Law* 863–78.

Cook, PJ and CM Carleton (eds.), *Continental Shelf Limits* (Oxford University Press: Oxford, 2000).

Chinese Society of International Law (CSIL), 'The South China Sea Arbitration Awards: A Critical Study' (2018) 17(2) *Chinese Journal of International Law* 207–748.

Davenport, T, 'Legal Implications of the South China Sea Award for Maritime Southeast Asia' (2016) 34 *Australian Yearbook of International Law* 65–86.

Fallon, T, 'The EU, the South China Sea and China's Successful Wedge Strategy', 13 October 2016, AMTI, available at, https://amti.csis.org/eu-south-china-sea-chinas-successful-wedge-strategy/.

Franckx, E, 'The Arbitral Tribunal's interpretatoion of paragraph 3 in Article 121: a first but important step forward' in S Jayakumar, T Koh, R Beckman, T Davenport and

HD Phan (eds), The South China Sea Arbitration: The Legal Dimension (Edward Elgar: Cheltenham, 2018), 154–175.

Freestone, D, 'International Law and Sea Level Rise' in RR Churchill and D Freestone (eds), *International Law and Global Climate Change* (Graham and Trotman/ Martinus Nijhoff: London/Dordrecht, 1991).

Freestone, D, 'Remarks by David Freestone', American Society of International Law (ASIL), 'The Regime of Islands in the Aftermath of the South China Sea Arbitration', ASIL 2017 Conference panel, *Proceedings of the Annual ASIL Meeting* 112 (Cambridge University Press: Cambridge, 2018).

Freestone, D and J Pethick, 'Sea Level Rise and Maritime Boundaries: International implications of impacts and responses', in GH Blake (ed.), *International Boundaries; Fresh Perspectives*, Volume 5 (Routledge: London, 1994) 73–90.

Freestone D and CH Schofield, 'Options to Protect Coastlines and Secure Maritime Jurisdictional Claims in the Face of Global Sea Level Rise' in M Gerrard and G Wannier (eds), *Threatened Island Nations: Legal Implications of Rising Seas and a Changing Climate*, (Cambridge University Press: Cambridge, 2013) 141–165.

Gau, MS, 'The Sino-Philippine Arbitration on the South China Sea Disputes and the Taiwan', (2016) 9(2) *Journal of East Asia and International Law* 479–496.

Geoscience Australia, 'Heard and McDonald Islands', available at https://www.ga.gov.au/scientific-topics/national-location-information/dimensions/remote-offshore-territories/heard-and-mcdonald-islands.

Gjetnes, M, 'The Spratlys: Are they Rocks or Islands?' (2010) 32 *Ocean Development and International Law* 191–204.

Gotev, G, 'EU unable to adopt statement upholding South China Sea ruling', *Euractiv*, 14 July 2016, available at https://www.euractiv.com/section/global-europe/news/eu-unable-to-adopt-statement-upholding-south-china-sea-ruling/.

Grossman, D, 'Why is China Pressing Indonesia Again Over Its Maritime Claims', *World Politics Review*, 16 January 2020, available at, https://www.worldpoliticsreview.com/articles/28476/why-is-china-pressing-indonesia-again-over-the-natuna-islands.

Gullett, WL, 'The South China Sea Arbitration's Contribution to the Concept of Juridical Islands' (2018) 47 *Questions of International Law* 5–38.

Gullett, WL and CH Schofield, 'Pushing the Limits of the Law of the Sea Convention: Australian and French Cooperative Surveillance and Enforcement in the Southern Ocean' (2007) 22(4) *International Journal of Marine and Coastal Law* 545–583.

Guilfoyle, D, 'Remarks by Douglas Guilfoyle', American Society of International Law (ASIL), 'The Regime of Islands in the Aftermath of the South China Sea Arbitration', ASIL 2017 Conference panel, *Proceedings of the Annual ASIL Meeting* 112 (Cambridge, Cambridge University Press, 2018).

Hancox D and JRV Prescott, *A Geographical Description of the Spratly Islands and An Account of Hydrographic Surveys Amongst Those Islands*, Maritime Briefing, 1(6) (International Boundaries Research Unit: Durham, 1995).

Hancox D and JRV Prescott, *Secret Hydrographic Surveys in the Spratly Islands*, (The Maritime Institute of Malaysia: Kuala Lumpur, 1997).

Hebert, J-L, 'The South China Sea Arbitration Award and Its Widespread Implications' (2018) 19(1) *Oregon Review of International Law* 289–314.

Hirst W and D Robertson, 'Geographic information systems, charts and UNCLOS: Can they live together?' (May-June 2004) 136 *Maritime Studies* 1–6.

Hodgson R, *Islands: Normal and Special Circumstances*, Research Study (U.S. Department of State, Bureau of Intelligence and Research: Washington D.C., 1973).

House of Commons (HC) *Hansard, Written Answers*, 21 July 1997, cols. 397–398.

Huang, K, 'Beijing marks out claims in South China Sea by naming geographical features', *South China Morning Post*, 20 April 2020, available at https://www.scmp.com/news/china/diplomacy/article/3080721/beijing-marks-out-claims-south-china-sea-naming-geographical.

International Court of Justice (ICJ), Statute of the International Court of Justice, available at https://www.icj-cij.org/en/statute.

International Hydrographic Organization (IHO) *A Manual on Technical Aspects of the United Nations Convention on the Law of the Sea – 1982 (TALOS)*, Special Publication No.51, 5th edition (International Hydrographic Bureau: Monaco, 2014).

International Law Commission (ILC), *Yearbook of the International Law Commission*, 1956, vol. II, available at http://legal.un.org/ilc/texts/instruments/english/commentaries/8_1_8_2_1956.pdf.

Intergovernmental Panel on Climate Change (IPCC), 'Special Report on the Ocean and Cryosphere in a Changing Climate', approved at its 51st Session, 20–23 September 2019, at 10, available at https://www.ipcc.ch/srocc/home/.

Jayewardene, HW, *The Regime of Islands in International Law* (Martinus Nijhoff: Dordrecht, 1990).

Jessup, PC, *The Law of Territorial Waters and Maritime Jurisdiction* (G.A, Jennings: New York, 1927).

Kashubsky, M, 'Protecting Offshore Oil and Gas Installations: Security Threats and Countervailing Measures' (August 2013) *Journal of Energy Security*, available at http://www.ensec.org/index.php?option=com_content&view=article&id=453:protecting-offshore-oil-and-gas-installations-security-threats-and-countervailing-measures&catid=137:issue-content&Itemid=422.

Kaye, SB, 'Assessing the Impact of the South China Sea Arbitration on Small Island States: A Case Study of Kiribati' (2019) 34(4) *International Journal of Marine and Coastal Law* 778–799.

Keating, SG, 'Rock of Island? It Was an UNCLOS Call: The Legal Consequence of Geospatial Intelligence to the 2016 South China Sea Arbitration and the Law of the Sea' (2018) 9 *Journal of National Security Law & Policy* 509–547.

Kenchington, R, "Maintaining Coastal and Lagoonal Ecosystems and Productivity" in H Terashima (ed.) *Proceedings of The International Symposium of Islands and Oceans* (Ocean Policy Research Foundation: Tokyo, 2009).

Klein, N, 'Islands and Rocks after the South China Sea Arbitration' (2016) 34 *The Australian Yearbook of International Law* 21–29.

Kohl, AW, 'China's Artificial Island Building Campaign in the South China Sea: Implications for the Reform of the Law of the Sea' (2018) 122 *Dickinson Law Review* 917–937.

Kraska, J, 'China's Maritime Militia Upends Rules on Naval Warfare', *The Diplomat*, 10 August 2015, available from http://thediplomat.com/2015/08/chinas-maritime-militia-upends-rules-on-naval-warfare/.

Kraska, J, 'The Struggle for Law in the South China Sea', paper presented at Seapower and Projection Forces in the South China Sea: Hearing before the Subcommittee on Seapower and Projection Forces of the Committee on Armed Services, House of Representatives, One Hundred Fourteenth Congress, Second Session, 21 September 2016 (W.S. Government Publishing Office: Washington D.C., 2018) 47–69.

Lewis, O, 'Remarks by Oliver Lewis', American Society of International Law (ASIL), 'The Regime of Islands in the Aftermath of the South China Sea Arbitration', ASIL 2017 Conference panel, *Proceedings of the Annual ASIL Meeting* 112 (Cambridge, Cambridge University Press, 2018).

Kwaitkowska, B, and AHA Soons, 'Entitlement to maritime areas of rocks which cannot sustain human habitation or economic life of their own' (1990) XXI *Netherlands Yearbook of International Law* 139–81.

Lathrop, CG, JA Roach and DR Rothwell (eds), 'Baselines under the International Law of the Sea: Reports of the International Law Association Committee on Baselines under the International Law of the Sea' (2019) 2(1–2) *Brill Research Perspectives on the Law of the Sea* 1–177.

Lavalle, R, 'Not Quite a Sure Thing: The Maritime Areas of Rocks and Low-tide Elevations Under the UN Law of the Sea Convention' (2004) 19(1) *International Journal of Marine and Coastal Law* 43–69.

Lavalle, R, 'The Rights of States over Low-tide Elevations: A Legal Analysis' (2014) 29 *International Journal of Marine and Coastal Law* 457–479.

Lu H and E Hou, 'Taiwan does not accept South China Sea ruling: President's Office', Focus Taiwan, CAN English News, 12 July 2016, available at https://focustaiwan.tw/politics/201607120024.

Lyons, Y, LQ Hung and P Tkalich, 'Determining high-tide features (or islands) in the South China Sea under Article 121(1): a legal and oceanography perspective', in

S Jayakumar, T Koh, R Beckman, T Davenport and HD Phan (eds), *The South China Sea Arbitration: The Legal Dimension* (Edward Elgar: Cheltenham, 2018) 128–153.

Mangosing, F, 'UK, Australia push for respect for rule of law, Hague ruling', Inquirer, 17 August 2018, available at https://globalnation.inquirer.net/169118/uk-australia-push-respect-rule-law-hague-ruling.

The Maritime Executive, 'Chinese Survey Vessel Returns to Disputed Vietnamese Waters', 15 April 2020, available at https://www.maritime-executive.com/article/chinese-survey-vessel-returns-to-disputed-vietnamese-waters.

MacDonald, F, 'The last outpost of Empire: Rockall and the Cold War' (2006) 32 *The Journal of Historical Geography* 627–647.

McDermott, L, 'Philippines v China – Rocks or Islands under International Law' (2017) 36(1), *University of Tasmania Law Review* 36–68.

McDorman, T, 'The South China Sea Arbitration' (2016) 20(17) *American Society of International Law Insights*, available at https://www.asil.org/insights/volume/20/issue/17/south-china-sea-arbitration.

Ministère de l'Intérieur, de l'Outre-Mer et des Collectivités territoriales, 'Les T.A.A.F.' available at: http://www.outre-mer.gouv.fr/outremer/front?id=outremer/decouvrir_outre_mer/taaf/publi_P_les_t_a_a_f_1082040279389.

Mossop, J, 'Remarks by Joanna Mossop', American Society of International Law (ASIL), 'The Regime of Islands in the Aftermath of the South China Sea Arbitration', ASIL 2017 Conference panel, *Proceedings of the Annual ASIL Meeting* 112 (Cambridge University Press: Cambridge, 2018).

Mossop, J, 'The South China Sea Arbitration and New Zealand's Maritime Claims' (2017) 15(2) *New Zealand Journal of Public International Law* 265–292.

Murphy, SD, *International Law relating to Islands*, Pocketbooks of the Hague Academy of International Law (Brill/Nijhoff: The Hague, 2017).

Nandan AN, and S Rosenne (eds.) *United Nations Convention on the Law of the Sea 1982: A Commentary*, Volumes II and III (Kluwer Law International: Dordrecht, 1995).

National Geographic, 'The Rock Cycle', available at, https://www.nationalgeographic.org/encyclopedia/rock-cycle/.

Navigation Guarantee Department of the Chinese Navy Headquarters, *China Sailing Directions: South China Sea* (A103) (2011).

Nordquist, MH, 'UNCLOS Article 121 and Itu Aba in the South China Sea Award: A correct interpretation?', in S Jayakumar, T Koh, R Beckman, T Davenport and Hao Duy Phan (eds), *The South China Sea Arbitration: The Legal Dimension* (Edward Elgar: Cheltenham, 2018) 176–204.

Oral, N, '"Rocks" or "Islands"?: Sailing Towards Legal Clarity in the Turbulent South China Sea', Symposium on the South China Sea Arbitration (2017) 110 *AJIL Unbound* 279–284.

Orstead, 'Our wind farms', available at https://orsted.co.uk/energy-solutions/offshore-wind.

Oude Elferink, AG, 'Clarifying Article 121 (3) of the Law of the Sea Convention: the limits set by the nature of international legal processes' (1998) 6(2) *Boundary and Security Bulletin* 58–68.

Oude Elferink, AG, 'The South China Sea Arbitration's Interpretation of Article 121(3) of the LOSC: A Disquieting First' *The JCLOS Blog*, 7 September 2016, available at file:///G:/My%20Drive/Research%20materials/South%20China%20Sea/The-South-China-Sea-Arbitrations-Interpretation-of-Article-1213-of-the-LOSC-A-Disquieting-First.pdf.

Oude Elferink, AG, 'The Russian Federation and the Arctic Sunrise Case: Hot Pursuit and Other Issues under the LOSC' (2016) 92 *International Legal Studies* 381–406.

Huang, K, 'Beijing marks out claims in South China Sea by naming geographical features', *The South China Morning Post*, 20 April 2020, available at https://www.scmp.com/news/china/diplomacy/article/3080721/beijing-marks-out-claims-south-china-sea-naming-geographical.

Jesus, JL 'Rocks, New-born Islands, Sea Level Rise and Maritime Space', in J Frowein *et al.* (eds) *Verhandeln für den Frieden: Negotiating for Peace* (Springer: Berlin, 2003) 579–603.

Oxman, BH, 'The South China Sea Arbitration Award', University of Miami Legal Studies Research Paper No. 16–41, 6 September 2016, available at SSRN, https://ssrn.com/abstract=2835534 or http://dx.doi.org/10.2139/ssrn.2835534.

tho Pesch, S, 'Coastal State Jurisdiction around Installations: Safety Zones in the Law of the Sea (2015) 30 *International Journal of Marine and Coastal Law* 512–532.

Prescott JRV and CH Schofield, *Maritime Political Boundaries of the World*, 2nd edition (Martinus Nijhoff: Leiden/Boston, 2005).

Reed, MW, *Shore and Sea Boundaries: The Development of International Maritime Boundary Principles through United States Practice*, Volume 3 (U.S. Department of Commerce, National Oceanic and Atmospheric Administration: Washington, DC, 2000).

Reuters, 'EU's statement on the South China Sea reflects divisions', *Reuters*, 15 July 2016, available at, https://www.reuters.com/article/southchinasea-ruling-eu/eus-statement-on-south-china-sea-reflects-divisions-idUSL8N1A130Y.

Roach, JA, 'Offshore Archipelagos Enclosed by Straight Baselines: An Excessive Claim?' (2018) 49 *Ocean Development and International Law* 176–202.

Roach, JA and RW Smith, *United States Responses to Excessive Maritime Claims*, 3rd edition (Martinus Nijhoff: Leiden, 2012).

Saunders, I, Artificial Islands and Territory in International Law' (2019) 52 *Vanderbilt Journal of International Law* 643–683.

Schofield, CH, 'Dangerous Ground – A Geopolitical Overview of the South China Sea in S Bateman and R Emmers (eds) *Security and International Politics in the South China Sea: Towards a Co-operative Management Regime* (Routledge: London, 2009) 7–25.

Schofield, CH, 'Islands or Rocks – Is that the Real Question?: The Treatment of Islands in the Delimitation of Maritime Boundaries' in MH Nordquist, JN Moore, AHA Soons and H-S Kim (eds), *The Law of the Sea Convention: US Accession and Globalization* (Martinus Nijhoff: Leiden/Boston, 2012) 322–340.

Schofield, CH, 'Defining the "Boundary" between Land and Sea: Territorial Sea Baselines in the South China Sea' in R Beckman, MR Page and L Bernard (eds) *UNCLOS and the South China Sea* (Edward Elgar: Cheltenham, 2014) 21–54.

Schofield, CH, 'Climate Change and Changing Coasts: Geophysical and Jurisdictional Implications of Sea Level Rise' (2017) 5(1) *Korean Journal of International and Comparative Law* 36–60.

Schofield, CH, 'An Incomplete Maritime Map: Progress and Challenges in the Delimitation of Maritime Boundaries in South East Asia' in D Rothwell and D Letts (eds) *Law of the Sea in South East Asia: Environmental, Navigational and Security Challenges* (Routledge: London, 2019) 33–62.

Schofield, CH, 'Contested ocean spaces: A case study of the South China Sea', *Geography Review* (November 2017) 31(2) 22–26.

Schofield, CH, 'Conflicting Maritime Visions of the South China Sea', *ASEAN Focus* (June 2020) 33(2) 15–17.

Schofield, CH and D Freestone, 'Islands Awash Amidst Rising Seas?: Sea Level Rise and Insular Status under the Law of the Sea' (2019) 34 *International Journal of Marine and Coastal Law* 391–414.

Schofield, CH and Arsana, IMA, 'Beyond the Limits?: Outer Continental Shelf Opportunities and Obligations in East and Southeast Asia', (2009) 31(1) *Contemporary Southeast Asia* 28–63.

Schofield, CH, JRV Prescott and R van de Poll, *An Appraisal of the Geographical Characteristics and Status of Certain Insular Features in the South China Sea* (March 2015).

Schofield, CH and RN Schofield, 'Testing the Waters: Charting the Evolution of Claims to and from Low-Tide Elevations and Artificial Islands Under the Law of the Sea' (2016) 1 *Asia-Pacific Journal for Ocean Law and Policy* 37–67.

Silverstein, AL, 'Okinotorishima: Artificial Preservation of a Speck of Sovereignty' (1990) 16(2) *Brooklyn Journal of International Law* 409–431.

Siregar, K, 'Indonesia deploys 4 additional warships to Natuna amid standoff with Chinese warships', *Channel News Asia*, 6 January 2020, available at, https://www.channelnewsasia.com/news/asia/indonesia-china-natuna-islands-dispute-south-china-sea-12237456?cid=h3_referral_inarticlelinks_24082018_cna.

Smith, R, 'Mapping the Islands of Quitasueño (Colombia) – Their Baselines, Territorial Sea, and Contiguous Zone', Expert report, February 2010.

Song, YH, 'The July 2016 Arbitration Award, Interpretation of Article 121(3) of the UNCLOS, and Selecting Examples of Inconsistent State Practices' (2018) 49 *Ocean Development and International Law* 247–261.

South China Morning Post, 'The South China Sea: Chinese ship Haiyang Dizhi 8 seen near Malaysian waters, security sources say', *South China Morning Post*, 18 April 2020, available at https://www.scmp.com/news/asia/southeast-asia/article/3080510/south-china-sea-chinese-ship-haiyang-dizhi-8-seen-near.

Stephens, T, 'The Collateral Damage from China's "Great Wall of Sand" – the Environmental Dimensions of the South China Sea Case' (2017) 17/06 *Sydney Law School, Legal Studies Research Paper*.

Straits Times, '5-nation face-off in high-seas energy tussle off Malaysia', *The Straits Times*, 25 April 2020, available at https://www.straitstimes.com/asia/se-asia/5-nation-face-off-in-high-seas-energy-tussle-off-malaysia.

Sumalia R, and W Cheung, *Boom or Bust: The Future of Fishing in the South China Sea* (ADM Capital Foundation, Hong Kong, 2015), available at http://www.admcf.org/wordpress/wp-content/uploads/2015/11/FishSCSea03_11-FINAL-FINAL.pdf.

Sweeney, S, 'Rocks v. Islands: Natural Tensions over Artificial Features in the South China Sea' (2017) 31 *Temple International & Comparative Law Journal* 599–634.

Symmons, CR, *The Maritime Zones of Islands in International Law* (Martinus Nijhoff: The Hague, 1979).

Symmons, CR, *Some Problems Relating to the Definition of Insular Features in International Law*, Maritime Briefing, 1(5) (International Boundaries Research Unit: Durham, 1995).

Symmons, CR, 'Ireland and the Rockall Dispute: An Analysis of Recent Developments', *Boundary and Security Bulletin* (1998) 6(1), 78–93.

Symmons, CR, *When is an 'Island' Not an 'Island' in International Law? The Riddle of Dinkum Sands in the Case of US v. Alaska*, Maritime Briefing, 2(6) (International Boundaries Research Uni:, Durham, 1999).

Talmon, S, 'Regime of Islands', in A Proelss (ed.), *United Nations on the Law of the Sea: A Commentary* (C.H. Beck/Hart/Nomos: Munich/Oxford/Baden-Baden, 2017) 858–880.

Talmon, S, 'The South China Sea Arbitration and the Finality of "Final" Awards' (2017) 8 *Journal of International Dispute* Settlement, 388–401.

Tanaka, Y, 'Reflections on the interpretation and Application of Article 121(3) in the South China Sea Arbitration (Merits)' (2017) 48(3–4) *Ocean Development and International Law* 365–385.

Tiezzi, S, 'Taiwan: South China Sea Ruling "Completely Unacceptable"', *The Diplomat*, 13 July 2016, available at https://thediplomat.com/2016/07/taiwan-south-china-sea-ruling-completely-unacceptable/.

Tsamenyi, BM, 'Managing Indonesian Traditional Fishing in Australian Waters: An Australian Perspective' 86 (1996) *Maritime Studies* 18–26.

Tsamenyi, BM, CH Schofield and B Milligan, 'Navigation through Archipelagos: Current State Practice', in MH Nordquist, TB Koh, and JN Moore (eds), *Freedom of the Seas, Passage Rights and the 1982 Law of the Sea Convention* (Martinus Nijhoff: Leiden/Boston, 2009) 413–454.

United Kingdom Hydrographic Office (UKHO) Admiralty Sailing Directions, *Pacific Islands Pilot*, NP60, Vol, 11th edition (UKHO: Taunton, 2007).

UKHO, *Admiralty Sailing Directions, China Sea Pilot*, NP30, Vol. 1, 8th edition (Taunton, UKHO, 2010).

United Nations, Division for Ocean Affairs and the Law of the Sea, *Régime of islands: Legislative history of Part VIII (Article 121) of the United Nations Convention on the Law of the Sea* (United Nations: New York, 1988).

United Nations, *Baselines: An Examination of the Relevant Provisions of the United Nations Convention on the Law of the Sea* (United Nations: New York, 1989).

United Nations Treaty Collection (UNTC), 'Status of Treaties: United Nations Convention on the Law of the Sea, Montego Bay, 10 December 1982', Declarations and Reservations, available at, https://treaties.un.org/Pages/ViewDetailsIII.aspx?src=TREATY&mtdsg_no=XXI-6&chapter=21&Temp=mtdsg3&clang=_en.

United Nations, *United Nations Conferences on the Law of the Sea, Official Records, Third Conference* (William S. Hein & Co: Buffalo, NY, 1980, reprinted 2000).

United States Department of State, *Developing Standard Guidelines for Evaluating Straight Baselines*, Limits in the Seas, No.106, (Bureau of Oceans and International Environmental and Scientific Affairs: Washington D.C., 31 August 1987).

United States Department of State, Bureau of Oceans and Environmental and Scientific Affairs, 'Straight Baseline Claim: China', *Limits in the Seas, No.117*, 1996, available at http://www.state.gov/documents/organization/57692.pdf.

Van Dyke, JM and RA Brooks, 'Uninhabited islands: their impact on the ownership of the oceans' resources' (1983) 12 *Ocean Development International Law Journal* 265–284.

Van Dyke, JM and D Bennett, Islands and the Delimitation of Ocean Space in the South China Sea' (1993) 10 *Ocean Yearbook* 54–89.

Van Dyke, JM, J Morgan and J Gurish, 'The exclusive economic zone of the northwestern Hawaiian Islands: When do uninhabited islands generate an EEZ?' (1988) 25(3) *San Diego Law Review* 425–494.

Vidas, D, D Freestone and J McAdam (eds), 'International Law and Sea Level Rise: Report of the International Law Association Committee on International Law and Sea Level Rise' (2019) 2(3) *Brill Research Perspectives on the Law of the Sea*.

Xin, L, 'Sansha city establishes two districts for better management', *Global Times*, 18 April 2020, available at, https://www.globaltimes.cn/content/1186004.shtml.

Zhang, F, 'Assessing China's response to the South China Sea arbitration ruling' (2017) 71(4) *Australian Journal of International Affairs* 440–459.

Treaties and Other International Instruments or National Official Documents

1930 Report of the Second Commission (Territorial Waters) of the Hague Codification Conference, Report of Sub-Committee II. See, Report of the Second Commission, L.N. Doc. C.230, M.117, 1930 V.

1958 Convention on the Territorial Sea and Contiguous Zone, opened for signature 29 April 1958, 516 U.N.T.S. 205 (entered into force 10 September 1964).

1958 Convention on the Continental Shelf, opened for signature 29 April 1958, 499 U.N.T.S. 311 (entered into force 10 June 1964).

1969 Vienna Convention on the Law of Treaties (VCLT), 23 May 1969 1155 UNTS 331 (entered into force 27 January 1980).

1981 Report and Recommendations to the Governments of Iceland and Norway of the Conciliation Commission on the Continental Shelf Area Between Iceland and Jan Mayen, June 1981 (1981) ILM 797–842.

1982 United Nations Convention on the Law of the Sea, 1833 UNTS 3.

1982 Agreement on Marine Delimitation between the Government of Australia and the Government of the French Republic, 4 January 1982 (in force 10 January 1983).

Mexico, Federal Act relating to the Sea, 8 January 1986, available at, http://www.un.org/Depts/los/LEGISLATIONANDTREATIES/PDFFILES/MEX_1986_Act.pdf.

2008 Japan, 'Japan's Submission to the Commission on the Limits of the Continental Shelf, Executive Summary', 12 November 2008, available at http://www.un.org/Depts/los/clcs_new/submissions_files/submission_jpn.htm.

2009 Brunei-Darussalam, 'Brunei-Darussalam's Preliminary Submission concerning the Outer Limits of its Continental Shelf', 12 May 2009, available at http://www.un.org/Depts/los/clcs_new/commission_preliminary.htm.

2009, Malaysia-Vietnam, 'Joint Submission by Malaysia and Socialist Republic of Viet Nam', Executive Summary (6 May 2009), available at http://www.un.org/Depts/los/clcs_new/submissions_files/submission_mysvnm_33_2009.htm.

2009, Vietnam, 'Outer Limits of the Continental Shelf beyond 200 Nautical Miles from the Baselines: Submission to the Commission: Submission by the Socialist Republic of Viet Nam', Executive Summary (7 May 2009), available at http://www.un.org/Depts/los/clcs_new/submissions_files/submission_vnm_37_2009.htm.

2009, China, Communications Received with regard to the Joint Submission made by Malaysia and Vietnam to the Commission on the Limits of the Continental Shelf, China (7 May 2009 and 14 April 2011).

2013 Philippines, 'Notification and Statement of Claim on the West Philippine Sea', 22 January 2013, available at http://www.pcacases.com/pcadocs/The%20

Philippines%27%20Memorial%20-%20Volume%20III%20%28Annexes%20 1-60%29.pdf.

2014 China, 'Position Paper on the Matter of Jurisdiction in the South China Sea Arbitration Initiated by the Republic of the Philippines', 7 December 2014, available on the website of the Ministry of Foreign Affairs of China available at www.fmprc .gov.cn/nanhai/eng/snhwtlcwj_1/t1368899.htm.

2015 China, 'Statement of the Ministry of Foreign Affairs on the Award on Jurisdiction and Admissibility of the South China Sea Arbitration by the Arbitral Tribunal Established at the Request of the Republic of the Philippines', 30 October 2015, on the Ministry of Foreign Affairs of China website available from www.fmprc.gov.cn/ mfa_eng/zxxx_662805/t1310474.shtml.

2016 China, 'Statement of the Ministry of Foreign Affairs of the People's Republic of China on the Award of 12 July 2016 of the Arbitral Tribunal in the South China Sea Arbitration Established at the Request of the Republic of the Philippines', https:// www.fmprc.gov.cn/mfa_eng/wjdt_665385/2649_665393/t1379492.shtml.

2016 Chinese (Taiwan) Society of International Law, 'Amicus Curiae Submission', 23 March 2016, available at csil.org.tw/home/wpcontent/uploads/2016/03/SCSTF -Amicus-Curiae-Brief-final.pdf.

2016 China 'Statement of the Ministry of Foreign Affairs on the Award of 12 July 2016 of the Arbitral Tribunal Established at the Request of the Republic of the Philippines', 12 July 2016, on the Ministry of Foreign Affairs of China website available at, www. fmprc.gov.cn/nanhai/eng/snhwtlcwj_1/t1379492.htm.

2016 Japan, Statement by Foreign Minister Fumio Kishida, 'Arbitration between the Republic of the Philippines and the People's Republic of China regarding the South China Sea (Final Award by the Arbitral Tribunal)', 12 July 2016, available at https:// www.mofa.go.jp/press/release/press4e_001204.html, (last accessed 30 July 2020).

2016 United Nations, S Dujarric, 'Remarks by Spokesperson for the U.N. Secretary-General on the South China Sea Arbitration', 12 July 2016, available at https://seas research.wordpress.com/2016/07/15/remarks-by-spokesperson-for-the-u-n -secretary-general-on-the-south-china-sea-arbitration/, (last accessed 29 July 2020).

2016 United States, J Kirby, 'Decision in the Philippines-China Arbitration', Press Statement, 12 July 2016, United States Department of State, available at https://2009-2017.state.gov/r/pa/prs/ps/2016/07/259587.htm.

2016 United States, United States Presidential Press Secretary also noted that the Tribunal's ruling is "final and binding." The White House, Press Briefing by Press Secretary Josh Earnest, 13 July 2016, available at https://obamawhitehouse .archives.gov/the-press-office/2016/07/13/press-briefing-press-secretary-josh -earnest-7132016, (last accessed 30 July 2020).

2016 Vietnam, 'Remarks of the Spokesperson of the Ministry of Foreign Affairs of Viet Nam on Viet Nam's reaction to the issuance of the Award by the Tribunal constituted under Annex VII to the United Nations Convention on the Law of the Sea in the arbitration between the Philippines and China', 12 July 2016, available at https://seasresearch.wordpress.com/2016/07/06/remarks-by-vietnams-mofa-spokesperson-on-vietnams-reaction-to-the-final-award-of-the-arbitration-case-initiated-by-the-philippines-against-china-by-the-permanent-court-of-arbitration/, (last accessed 30 July 2020).

2016 New Zealand, Government of New Zealand, Foreign Minister Murray McCully, 'NZ comment on South China Sea Tribunal ruling', 13 July 2016, available at https://www.beehive.govt.nz/release/nz-comment-south-china-sea-tribunal-ruling?utm_source=feedburner&utm_medium=feed&utm_campaign=Feed%3A+beehive-govt-nz%2Fportfolio%2Fforeign-affairs+%28Foreign+Affairs+-+beehive.govt.nz%29, (last accessed 30 July 2020).

2016 Canada, Global Affairs Canada, Statement by Honourable Stéphane Dion, Minister of Foreign Affairs, 'Canadian Statement on South China Sea Arbitration', 21 July 2016, available at https://www.canada.ca/en/global-affairs/news/2016/07/canadian-statement-on-south-china-sea-arbitration.html, (last accessed 30 July 2020).

2016 ASEAN, 'Joint Communiqué of the 49th ASEAN Foreign Ministers' Meeting', 25 July 2016, available at https://asean.org/joint-communique-of-the-49th-asean-foreign-ministers-meeting/.

2016, the Philippines, Republic of the Philippines, Department of Foreign Affairs, 'Information Note on the Significance of the 2016 ASEAN Joint Communiqué in Relation to the Arbitral Tribunal Ruling', 1 August 2016, available at https://www.dfa.gov.ph/newsroom/dfa-releases/10072-information-note-on-the-significance-of-the-2016-asean-joint-communique-in-relation-to-the-arbitral-tribunal-ruling.

2016 China, 'Statement of the Ministry of Foreign Affairs of the People's Republic of China on the Award of 12 July 2016 of the Arbitral Tribunal in the South China Sea Arbitration Established at the Request of the Republic of the Philippines', https://www.fmprc.gov.cn/mfa_eng/wjdt_665385/2649_665393/t1379492.shtml.

2017 Australia-Japan-United States, Joint Statement by the Foreign Ministers of Australia and Japan together with the Secretary of State of the United States. The Ministers made their joint statement following the seventh ministerial meeting of the Trilateral Strategic Dialogue (TSD) on 7 August 2017, available at https://www.state.gov/r/pa/prs/ps/2017/08/273216.htm, (last accessed 30 July 2020).

2019 Malaysia, 'Malaysia Partial Submission', Executive Summary (12 December 2019), available at https://www.un.org/Depts/los/clcs_new/submissions_files/mys85_2019/20171128_MYS_ES_DOC_001_secured.pdf.

2020 China, Communication Received with regards to the submission made by Malaysia, China (23 March 2020), available at https://www.un.org/Depts/los/clcs_new/submissions_files/submission_mys_12_12_2019.html.

2020 The Philippines, Communication Received with regards to the submission made by Malaysia, The Philippines (6 March, communication 2), available at https://www.un.org/Depts/los/clcs_new/submissions_files/submission_mys_12_12_2019.html.

2020 Vietnam, Communication Received with regards to the submission made by Malaysia, Vietnam (30 March and 10 April), available at https://www.un.org/Depts/los/clcs_new/submissions_files/submission_mys_12_12_2019.html.

2020, Indonesia, Communication Received with regards to the submission made by Malaysia, Indonesia (26 May).

2020 United States, Communications Received with regards to the submission made by Malaysia, United States (1 June), available at https://www.un.org/Depts/los/clcs_new/submissions_files/submission_mys_12_12_2019.html.

2020 Australia, Communications Received with regards to the submission made by Malaysia, Australia (23 July), available at https://www.un.org/Depts/los/clcs_new/submissions_files/submission_mys_12_12_2019.html.

2020 United States-Australia, United States Department of State, 'Joint Statement on Australia-U,S, Ministerial consultations (AUSMIN) 2020', Media Note, 28 July 2020, available at https://www.state.gov/joint-statement-on-australia-u-s-ministerial-consultations-ausmin-2020/.

Cases

1984 Delimitation of the Maritime Boundary in the Gulf of Maine Area (Canada/United States of America), Judgment of [1984] ICJ Reports, 246, ICGJ 120, 12 October 1984 International Court of Justice [ICJ].

1993 *Case Concerning maritime Delimitation in the Area between Greenland and Jan Mayen* (Denmark v. Norway), Judgment, ICJ Reports, 38, ICGJ 94, 14 June 1993, International Court of Justice [ICJ].

1996 Supreme Court of the United States (March 1996) No. 84 (Original) (*Report of the Special Master*).

2000 *The 'Monte Confurco' Case* (*Seychelles v France*), ITLOS Case No 6, ICGJ 339Judgment, 18 December 2000, Declaration of Judge Vukas, International Tribunal on the Law of the Sea [ITLOS].

2001 *Case Concerning Maritime Delimitation and Territorial Questions between Qatar and Bahrain* (Qatar v. Bahrain) (Merits) [2001] ICJ Reports, 40.

2002 *The "Volga" Case* (*Russian Federation v. Australia*) (Prompt Release) (2002) ITLOS Case No. 11, ICGJ 344, 23 December 2002, Declaration of Vice-President Vukas, International Tribunal on the Law of the Sea [ITLOS].

Land and Maritime Boundary between Cameroon and Nigeria (Cameroon v. Nigeria; Equatorial Guinea intervening), [2002] *ICJ Reports* 303, ICGJ 63, 10 October 2002, International Court of Justice [ICJ].

2006 *Barbados/Trinidad and Tobago Arbitration*, Award of the Arbitral Tribunal, 45 ILM 839, ICGJ 371 11 April 2006, Permanent Court of Arbitration [PCA].

2007 In the Matter of an Arbitration between Guyana and Suriname, Award of the Arbitral Tribunal, ICGJ 370, PCA Case No 2004–04, 17 September 2007, Permanent Court of Arbitration [PCA].

2007 *Territorial and Maritime Dispute between Nicaragua and Honduras in the Caribbean Sea* (Nicaragua v. Honduras), Judgment, [2007] ICJ Reports 2007, 659, ICGJ 23, 8 October 2007, International Court of Justice [ICJ].

2008 *Case concerning Sovereignty over Pedra Branca/Pulau Batu Puteh, Middle Rocks and South Ledge* (Malaysia/Singapore), Judgment. ICGJ 9, 23 May 2008, International Court of Justice [ICJ].

2009 *Case Concerning Maritime Delimitation in the Black Sea* (Romania v. Ukraine), Judgment, [2009] ICJ Reports 61, ICGJ 6, 3 February 2009, International Court of Justice [ICJ].

2009 In the Matter of an Arbitration under the Arbitration Agreement between the Government of the Republic of Croatia and the Government of the Republic of Slovenia, signed on 4 November 2009, Final Award, PCA Case No. 2012–04, 29 June 2017, Permanent Court of Arbitration [PCA].

2012 *Dispute Concerning Delimitation of the Maritime Boundary between Bangladesh and Myanmar in the Bay of Bengal (Bangladesh/Myanmar)*, International Tribunal for the Law of the Sea (ITLOS), Case no.16, Judgment, 14 March 2012.

2012 *Territorial and Maritime Dispute (Nicaragua v Colombia)*, Judgment, [2012] ICJ Reports 50, ICGJ 426 19 November 2012, International Court of Justice [ICJ].

2015 *The Arctic Sunrise Arbitration* (Netherlands v. Russian Federation), Case No. 2014–02, Award on the Merits, 14 August 2015, Permanent Court of Arbitration [PCA].

2016 *South China Sea Arbitration, Philippines v China*, Award, PCA Case No 2013–19, ICGJ 495 (PCA 2016), 12 July 2016, Permanent Court of Arbitration [PCA].

www.ingramcontent.com/pod-product-compliance
Lightning Source LLC
Chambersburg PA
CBHW071351230926
51846CB00002B/510
9789004449466